SpringerBriefs in Law

SpringerBriefs present concise summaries of cutting-edge research and practical applications across a wide spectrum of fields. Featuring compact volumes of 50 to 125 pages, the series covers a range of content from professional to academic. Typical topics might include:

- A timely report of state-of-the art analytical techniques
- A bridge between new research results, as published in journal articles, and a contextual literature review
- A snapshot of a hot or emerging topic
- A presentation of core concepts that students must understand in order to make independent contributions

SpringerBriefs in Law showcase emerging theory, empirical research, and practical application in Law from a global author community. SpringerBriefs are characterized by fast, global electronic dissemination, standard publishing contracts, standardized manuscript preparation and formatting guidelines, and expedited production schedules.

Stephan Koloßa

Whistleblower Protection and the Right of Access

Synthesising the EU Whistleblower Directive and Art. 15 GDPR

Springer

Stephan Koloßa
Technical University of Munich
Munich, Germany

Technical University of Braunschweig
Brunswick, Germany

ISSN 2192-855X ISSN 2192-8568 (electronic)
SpringerBriefs in Law
ISBN 978-3-032-04816-5 ISBN 978-3-032-04817-2 (eBook)
https://doi.org/10.1007/978-3-032-04817-2

The original submitted manuscript has been translated into English. The translation was done using artificial intelligence. A subsequent revision was performed by the author(s) to further refine the work and to ensure that the translation is appropriate concerning content and scientific correctness. It may, however, read stylistically different from a conventional translation.

This Springer imprint is published by the registered company Springer Nature Switzerland AG.
The registered company address is: Gewerbestrasse 11, 6330 Cham, Switzerland

Acknowledgements The idea for this book originated while pursuing my LL. M. degree in Legal Tech at the University of Regensburg. Completing the master programme, finishing my thesis as well as developing it into an actual book would not have been possible without the support and encouragement of a few people, to whom I would like to express my deepest gratitude.

I would like to thank my supervisor, Prof. Dr. Frank Maschmann (University of Regensburg), for his helpful feedback and support throughout this project. His expertise and guidance were instrumental in shaping both the direction and the quality of my work.

I am also grateful to my superiors in academia, especially Prof. Dr. Dirk Heckmann (Technical University of Munich) and Prof. Dr. Anne Paschke (Technical University of Braunschweig), who contributed to the realization of this project by providing a rich and inspiring environment for my research.

Deepest thanks are also due to my learned colleague Dr. Laura Hofmann (Springer). Beyond that I am grateful for friends and supporters, in particular Gabrielle Schillinger who massively improved the language and readability of this book.

Finally, my heartfelt thanks go to my family, especially Dr. Judit Beke-Martos whose patience and constant encouragement kept me going through the challenges and triumphs of this journey. Their belief in me has been my greatest motivation.

Competing Interests The author has no competing interests to declare that are relevant to the content of this manuscript.

Contents

Chapter 1
Introduction

The past has shown that fraudulent schemes both in the business context and in the public sector, often remain undetected and without consequence for a significant period of time. This is also true for situations in which the misconduct occurs on a large scale. In the case of the so-called Panama Papers, the Panamanian law firm Mossack Fonseca assisted various public figures like politicians, football officials, billionaire entrepreneurs and celebrities in illegally moving their money out of the reach of the tax authorities of that state where they gained their profits.[1] Only after a whistleblower provided the Süddeutsche Zeitung (SZ) with over eleven million incriminating documents, did the schemes come to light. In the Wirecard case, in which the company manipulated balance sheets and conducted sham transactions on a large scale, the whistleblower Pav Gill, played a crucial role in uncovering the criminal actions.[2] The report in the "LuxLeaks" case, which contributed to the exposure of controversial Luxembourg tax saving models, even led the whistleblower to the European Court of Human Rights (ECHR) in Strasbourg.[3] Whistleblowers play an important role in combating these schemes. The data protection right to information has at least the potential, however, to significantly undermine the protection of whistleblowers. A careful balance is of utmost importance.

[1] The case has been described in various articles such as: Washington Post, Billions hidden beyond reach (2021); ZeitOnline, Millions in additional tax revenue through Panama Papers evaluation (2021).

[2] Wirecard whistleblower reveals himself, FAZ (2021).

[3] ECtHR Judg. of 11.5.2021–21884/18, Halet against Luxembourg.

S. Koloßa, *Whistleblower Protection and the Right of Access*, SpringerBriefs in Law,
https://doi.org/10.1007/978-3-032-04817-2_1

1.1 Thematic Introduction—Legal Background

The legal protection of whistleblowers is essential for a functioning whistleblower system. Whistleblowers, like those in the cases mentioned above, are not deserters, they often fulfil an important role and have a necessary function. Without legal protection, probably no one would seriously consider reporting unlawful activities or raising their voice against criminal behaviour and bringing it to light. Probably true also that the larger and more encompassing the scheme, the less likely it is to be reported. The fear of discrimination, reprisals, and other serious backlashes leading to disadvantages would be far too great for those who would speak, unless a functioning system of protection is in place.

A precise hint about a misconduct is often related to specific individuals rather than the abstract without connection to anyone. The facts of a case may concern a member of the top management, a supervisor, or a colleague as another employee. Once a person is suspected in the context of a whistleblower report, an appropriate investigation usually takes place against them. In this context, the whistleblower is only comprehensively protected if their identity is kept strictly confidential.

At the same time, data protection has—rightly so—taken on an important role as an expression of the right to informational self-determination, i.e. the right to generally be able to have access to one's data and to dispose of them. As such, data protection law tends to have a far reach whereby the individual gains largely effective power over their data. Some go as far as to claim data protection as a modern "superior fundamental right".[4] A core component of data protection is the claim of the concerned person for information about their data. Through this claim, the individual is only able to assert further rights such as the right to data correction or data deletion, as they only know which data about them is stored and processed.[5] This right to information also strengthens the principle of transparency within the meaning of Art. 12 GDPR.[6] It is therefore the most basic right among the affected data protection rights. This right reaches far enough to provide access to otherwise confidential information, hence, for example the status of an internal investigation or specifically the identity of a whistleblower who made serious accusations, could also be sought and the right to information would normally provide the requesting individual with all this data.

If a concerned person asserts their right of access under Art. 15 GDPR and demands the disclosure of the identity of the whistleblower, especially while the internal investigations are still ongoing, the employer is in a dilemma. Does he grant the person who makes the request for information, access to the identity of

[4] See e.g. Müller (2013), rather rejecting this position: Kelber (2022), p. 139; Smoltczyk, Kugelmann (2021).

[5] Paal, Nikol (2022), p. 467.

[6] Scientific Service of the German Parliament (Bundestag), The protection of informants ("whistleblowers") in Germany, p. 6.

the whistleblower and thus delivers the whistleblower person? Or does he protect the whistleblower, refuses to provide information about their identity and thereby possibly violates data protection law?

1.2 Aim of the Work and the Underlying Question

This work examines exactly that dilemma of the employer, when the obligation to provide access under Art. 15 GDPR and the obligation to protect the identity of the whistleblower collide. It answers the question of whether and under what conditions the employer must comply with a request for access. In the hypothetical situation, in which the employer receives information via an internal reporting channel, it is at the same time responsible for the protection of all concerned data and with that is the addressee of the request by the holder of the right of access. The employer is the only one who knows the identity of the whistleblower. At the same time, both affected parties, the whistleblower, as well as the person requesting information on the whistleblower, are employees of the employer.

In some ways, the present work is limited in its scope. On the one hand, it focuses mainly on an internal whistleblower report. In whistleblower situations, one can generally distinguish between internal and external hints or internal and external whistleblowing. Internal whistleblowing in the corporate context includes the case where the whistleblower turns to a company-internal office set up specifically for this purpose and gives his hint there alone. In external whistleblowing, the whistleblower does not directly turn to the general public, but rather to public authorities. Accordingly, the work hereinafter is premised on an internal whistleblower report.

On the other hand, the work highlights the data protection right to access specifically regarding the disclosure of the identity of the person, who provides the information, in relation to the protection of such a person. It takes only European Union law and European law into account, with special emphasis on legal requirements derived from the relevant conventions. The contents of national statutes such as the German Whistleblower Protection Act of 2023 are not covered by this work. Further jurisprudence, in particular of Germany, is also taken into account, yet mainly to draw general conclusions without exclusively focusing on German law.

Chapter 2 examines the protection of the whistleblower's identity's confidentiality, while Chap. 3 deals with the conditions of the data protection right to information about the origin of his data. Chapter 4 includes the balancing act to reconcile both interests. The Conclusion provides a brief final evaluation and an outlook.

References

Academic Articles and Contributions

Paal B, Nikol D (2022) On the identification of whistleblowers in the tension between the Whistleblower Protection Act. Whistleblow Direct Gener Data Protect Regul Compl Adv 466

Court Decisions

ECtHR Judg. of 11 May 2021–21884/18, Halet against Luxembourg

(Official) Documents

Kelbe U (2022) Editorial, data protection news. Available at https://www.datenschutzverein.de/wp-content/uploads/2022/10/DANA_22_3_Sonderheft_Datenschutz_und_andere_Grundrechte.pdf. Last Accessed 14 Sep 2025

Scientific Service of the German Parliament (Bundestag) (2019) The protection of informants ("whistleblowers") in Germany. WD 7–3000–257/18

Smoltczyk M, Kugelmann D (2021) Position paper 711.437.2. Available at https://www.datenschutz-berlin.de/fileadmin/user_upload/pdf/pressemitteilungen/2021/2021-BlnBDI-LfdRLP-Standpunkt_Attacke_auf_Datenschutz.pdf. Last Accessed 14 Sep 2025

Newspaper Articles

FAZ (2021) Wirecard whistleblower reveals himself, 20 June 2021. Available at https://www.faz.net/aktuell/wirtschaft/wirecard-whistleblower-enttarnt-sich-17350667.html. Last Accessed 14 Sep 2025

Müller R (2013) Super fundamental right to data protection, faz.net from 19 July 2013. Available at https://www.faz.net/aktuell/politik/staat-und-recht/bundesverfassungsgericht-supergrundrecht-datenschutz-12286801.html. Last Accessed 14 Sep 2025

Washington Post (2021) Billions hidden beyond reach, 3 Oct 2021. Available at https://www.washingtonpost.com/business/interactive/2021/pandora-papers-offshore-finance/. Last Accessed 14 Sep 2025

ZeitOnline (2021) Millions in additional tax revenue through Panama papers evaluation, 16 Feb 2021. Available at https://www.zeit.de/wirtschaft/2021-02/steuerhinterziehung-panama-papers-einnahmen-bund-millionen. Last Accessed 14 Sep 2025

Chapter 2
Protection of Whistleblowers' Confidentiality Under European Law

In recent years, the number of illegal actions in particular at the corporate level has grown, or at least the number of cases that came to light, increased.[1] Such misconduct has often only been exposed because brave informants have risked a great deal in order to put an end to it. Hence, it is no surprise that whistleblower protection has come into focus. If violations of law and order go undetected and unpunished for years because employees of a company fear to report illegal activities for fear of reprisals or consequences, it can have several negative effects. It can harm the company itself, but also third-parties, the economy in general, public procurement programs, the general public, and even the rule of law could be affected.[2] Protecting those who would assist in reducing unlawful or even criminal behaviour has two main functions: Protecting the individual's actions as well as protecting the public good. A well-balanced whistleblower protection may have positive effects on both of these.

If a whistleblower enjoys effective protection, that may also represent a kind of particular deterrence because, in a way, abusive behaviour or misconduct is then realistically threatened to be exposed; actions lie under Damocles' sword. People who engage in such unlawful behaviour feel less secure that their actions would not face consequences, knowing or trusting that no one would risk reporting them. In addition to the particular deterrence objective, whistleblower protection also has a generally deterrent character. Such far-reaching whistleblower protection may also serve that region as a strong, candid business location. If the employer's or their representatives' supposedly punishable behaviour can be reported through a criminal complaint to the public prosecutor's office, that can serve the perception of civic rights. Whistleblower protection thus also serves to secure the rule of law.

---

[1] For a specific sectoral overview on the field of research, see e.g. Leclerc (2023).

[2] See e.g. Martić (2021).

S. Koloßa, *Whistleblower Protection and the Right of Access*, SpringerBriefs in Law,
https://doi.org/10.1007/978-3-032-04817-2_2

Some voices even claim that whistleblowing is not only a legal right but a civic duty.[3] Only then would it be possible to bring real change and disclose wrongdoing in the interest of the public. According to this view, whistleblowing would be a civic duty just as the protection and defence of the rule of law, human rights or democracy.[4] However, in legal terms, whistleblowing is not an obligation of the employee and thus cannot be treated as such in the legal context.

The key element in the whistleblower protection is keeping the whistleblower's identity confidential.[5] However, and especially considering the aforementioned aims and principles, protecting the whistleblower's identity, cannot be absolute. Such a far-reaching mechanism would undermine the affected person's rights as well as give the person filing a report about an alleged misconduct the chance to abuse the mechanism and make unjustified allegations or take revenge at a disliked person De Sousa (2020). Therefore, the First Chapter sheds light on the existing legal whistleblower protection on a European level while focusing particularly on the basic requirements of the whistleblower status and the limits on the protection of a whistleblower's identity.

Whistleblower protection is now a firm part of both law of international conventions and EU law. At the level of international conventions, whistleblowers have been granted protection by various conventions created under the auspices of the Council of Europe and are particularly protected by the human right to freedom of expression under Art. 10 Convention for the Protection of Human Rights and Fundamental Freedoms (ECHR) (**see 2.1.**). At the EU level, whistleblower protection is primarily anchored in EU Directive 2019/1937 (the so-called Whistleblower Protection Directive or Whistleblower Directive) (**see 2.2.**).

2.1 Protection of Whistleblowers Under the Council of Europe

The need for sufficiently protecting whistleblowers in Europe has been present for a long time. The Council of Europe, a voluntary international organization with currently 46 member states, supported international conventions that included a minimum level of whistleblower protection and has over time launched several initiatives to help whistleblower protection become more effective (**see 2.1.1.**). Furthermore, the Convention for the Protection of Human Rights and Fundamental Freedoms also protects the whistleblower through the right to freedom of expression (**see 2.1.2.**).

---

[3] Kostakopoulou (2024).

[4] Kostakopoulou (2024), p. 477.

[5] Cf. European Data Protection Supervisor, Whistleblowing (2025); Stappers (2021), p. 95.

2.1.1 *Whistleblower Protection at the Level of the Council of Europe*

Within the Council of Europe, several initiatives have been launched to protect whistleblowers.[6] Not all of these initiatives are binding, nor are they directly and broadly applicable statutory acts. Nevertheless, they have played a meaningful role in the evolution of the whistleblower protection laws in Europe including that of the European Union.

2.1.1.1 Civil and Criminal Law Conventions on Corruption

The idea to protect whistleblowers from repercussions or other disadvantages by statutory law is not an entirely new one. However, at the Council of Europe there has only been a sectoral approach for a long time. It has been seen essentially as part of the fight against corruption.

The Civil Law Convention on Corruption is the Council of Europe's first attempt to define common international rules in the field of civil law and corruption.[7] One of the main aims of this convention was to create and install effective remedies for persons having suffered damages resulting from acts of corruption, to enable them to defend their rights and interests, and in particular to obtain compensation.[8] It entered into force in 2003, and thus far, it has been ratified by and is in force in 34 states.[9] Compliance with this convention is monitored by the Group of States against Corruption (GRECO).[10] Art. 9 Civil Law Convention on Corruption foresees that "[e]ach Party shall provide in its internal law for appropriate protection against any unjustified sanction for employees who have reasonable grounds to suspect corruption and who report in good faith their suspicion to responsible persons or authorities." The wording of Art. 9 Civil Law Convention on Corruption corresponds with Art. 33 United Nations Convention against Corruption.[11] The main elements for the scope of protection of a later to–be-

[6] This list of initiatives and sectoral approaches to whistleblower protection is not comprehensive. Other sectoral regulation on whistleblower protection can be found in Steinhauser, Kreis (Steinhauser and Kreis 2021), p. 425.

[7] Civil Law Convention on Corruption, European Treaty Series No. 174, entered into force on 01.11.2003, further information on status and ratifications, see: https://www.coe.int/en/web/impact-convention-human-rights/civil-law-convention-on-corruption#/ (last accessed: 14.09.2024).

[8] Art. 1 Civil Law Convention on Corruption.

[9] See on these details the Treaty Office of the Council of Europe: https://www.coe.int/fr/web/conventions/full-list?module=treaty-detail&treatynum=174 (last accessed: 14.09.2024).

[10] Group of States against Corruption, see: https://www.coe.int/en/web/greco/home (last accessed: 14.09.2024).

[11] Art. 33 United Nations Convention against Corruption: "Each State Party shall consider incorporating into its domestic legal system appropriate measures to provide protection against any unjustified treatment for any person who reports in good faith and on reasonable grounds to

called whistleblower are already visible in these relevant provisions, namely that the grounds provided for the suspicion are reasonable and the reporting person acts in good faith. Although the exact meaning of these two elements remains unclear, they have served as a useful basis for the development of the protection of whistleblowers.

The Criminal Law Convention on Corruption[12] prescribes in its Art. 22.a that "[e]ach Party shall adopt such measures as may be necessary to provide effective and appropriate protection for [. . .] those who report the criminal offences established in accordance with Art. 2 to 14 or otherwise co-operate with the investigating or prosecuting authorities". Unfortunately, this convention that has been ratified by 46 states and entered into force in 2002 after 14 ratifications, only calls for an effective and appropriate protection without addressing any further requirements.

2.1.1.2 The Seventh General Activity Report of the Group of States Against Corruption (GRECO) 2006

This report was a reaction to the various previous scandals, primarily involving Enron, WorldCom, and Parmalat.[13] The US-based Enron Corporation was engaged in a large-scale fraud scheme that involved accounting fraud and resulted in Enron's bankruptcy.[14] Similarly, the telecommunication company WorldCom was also engaged in accounting fraud, when it came to light that the company had overstated assets by 11 billion US Dollars.[15] In the latter case, the whistleblower Kim Emigh was ultimately fired for reporting the misconduct.[16] Italy's food manufacturer Parmalat caused a comparable scandal, which is accordingly often referred to as the European Enron case. The accounting fraud in the Parmalat case concerned about 14 billion Euros in overstatements of assets.[17] After these large-scale cases of mismanagement, the GRECO reacted in an attempt to foster whistleblower protection.

During its 32nd Plenary Meeting in 2007, the GRECO adopted the Seventh General Activity Report of 2006 and included a large section exclusively on the

the competent authorities any facts concerning offences established in accordance with this Convention."; United Nations Convention against Corruption, United Nations Treaty Series No. 2349, entered into force on 14.12.2005, see also: https://www.unodc.org/documents/brussels/UN_Convention_Against_Corruption.pdf (last accessed: 14.09.2024).

[12] Criminal Law Convention on Corruption, European Treaty Series No. 173, entered into force on 01.07.2002, further information on status and ratifications, see: https://www.coe.int/en/web/impact-convention-human-rights/criminal-law-convention-on-corruption#/ (last accessed: 14.09.2024).

[13] Seventh General Activity Report, Para. XV. Introduction, p. 10.

[14] See e.g. Bondarenko (Bondarenko).

[15] George (2021).

[16] George (2021).

[17] Cambanza (2024).

protection of whistleblowers. In the report, the GRECO highlighted that one of the most effective means against corruption is the realistic fear of being caught.[18] This situation may only be fostered, if a person willing to make a report, does not avoid any confrontation due to serious concerns of repercussions or sanctions. Interestingly, the report also foresaw the potential dilemma between the protection of whistleblowers and the protection of personal data, including the need for reconciliation.

The GRECO highlighted in its recommendation that it would not be enough simply to protect employees from being disciplined or dismissed for filing reports as there were more subtle forms of retribution.[19] Whistleblowers would need advice, while employers would need procedures and guidelines on how to properly file a report. Also, potential contradictions between the whistleblowing and the obligation to keep such information confidential must be addressed by proper laws, including enforceable guarantees. Overall, any and all whistleblowing laws must be properly promulgated through the adequate legislative body. The report also emphasized that a whistleblower was in need of protection regardless of whether he or she acted in a public or private setting.[20]

The GRECO elaborated on the prerequisites of whistleblower protection. Whistleblowing should be possible both internally and towards an external third party.[21] Any report must be based on a sufficient degree of suspicion. For an internal report, a genuine suspicion would meet the requirement of sufficiency, whereas the suspicion to an external regulator must be slightly higher and meet the threshold of reasonability.[22]

On the question of how to ensure a whistleblower's confidentiality, the report firstly acknowledged the distinction between confidentiality and anonymity of a whistleblower.[23] A whistleblower is anonymous, if nothing is known about his or her identity. As the GRECO correctly emphasised, entirely anonymous complaints are harder to investigate and may even be a "cloak for malice".[24] Therefore, non-anonymous complaints are much more desirable. However, not only the name of the whistleblower needed protection since his or her identity might also be revealed by the circumstances of the case. An effective protection of the whistleblower's confidentiality therefore requires more than simply redacting his or her name from the files.

In order to trigger protective means, the whistleblower must act in good faith. In its report, the GRECO described this requirement as absolutely necessary in order to reduce the risk of abuse or misuse through filing a report. "Good faith" does not

---

[18] Seventh General Activity Report, Para. XV. Introduction, p. 10.

[19] Seventh General Activity Report, Para. XV. Introduction, p. 10.

[20] Seventh General Activity Report, Para. XV. Introduction, p. 11.

[21] Seventh General Activity Report, Para. XV. Introduction, p. 12.

[22] Seventh General Activity Report, Para. XV. Introduction, p. 12.

[23] Seventh General Activity Report, Para. XV. Introduction, p. 12.

[24] Seventh General Activity Report, Para. XV. Introduction, p. 12.

mean that the whistleblower must act "honestly" or that his or her motives would need to be entirely virtuous.[25] Neither is there a need for the reported information to be objectively correct. Liberating the whistleblower from making sure all details are correct is important because they could only ascertain all of these if they were to conduct an investigation on their own prior to filing a report and that should not be an obligation on the whistleblower. Hence, even if a report was made in explicit bad faith, for example because the reporting person held a grudge against the affected person, such reporting would also trigger the whistleblower's protection if and as long as the reported incident was in the public interest. Although the GRECO did not come to a concise conclusion on what a most effective whistle-blower protection looked like, it did shed light and elaborate on some of the most imminent questions.

2.1.1.3 Motion for a Recommendation for the Protection of Whistleblowers (2007)

On 23 April 2007, a group of the members of the Council of Europe's Parliamentary Assembly, led by Mr. Bartumeu Cassany presented a motion for a recommendation on the protection of whistleblowers. The motion's primary focus was the protection of persons from possible disciplinary or criminal sanctions, who disclosed illegal activities of state organs.[26] The motion specifically referenced the Seventh General Activity Report of the GRECO adopted in 2007 as well as Art. 9 of the Civil Law Convention on Corruption. The motion explicitly stated that the existing rudimentary whistleblower protection mechanisms had not yet been enough to "break the rule of silence"[27] in their current state "the factual protective means would lack effectiveness."[28] Through this motion, the topic of effective whistleblower protection was once again highlighted and awarded more public attention. Unfortunately, the motion was not particularly specific, it was merely a general call for more whistleblower protection.

2.1.1.4 Report 12006 of the Protection of Whistleblowers (2009)

On 14 September 2009, the rapporteur Mr. Pieter Omtzigt reported to the Council of Europe's Committee on Legal Affairs and Human Rights about the importance of a more effective protection mechanism of whistleblowers. Subsequently, he presented what was later adopted as Resolution 1729 by the Parliamentary Assembly of the Council of Europe. Overall, Mr. Omtzigt's

---

[25] Seventh General Activity Report, Para. XV. Introduction, p. 13.

[26] Motion for a recommendation on the protection of whistleblowers (Cassany 2007), para. 1.

[27] Motion for a recommendation on the protection of whistleblowers (Cassany 2007), para. 4.

[28] Motion for a recommendation on the protection of whistleblowers (Cassany 2007), para. 5.

report emphasized that the protection should be granted only to those persons who make a report in good faith.[29] A person is assumed to act in good faith if he or he has reasonable grounds to believe the reported information to be true.[30] Such definition of good faith had been lacking before, as the earlier discussion had either been on the veracity of the information given or the motives pursued by the whistleblower.[31] The report claimed that if the purported whistleblower made false accusations intentionally or recklessly, then that person should not benefit from any special protection and should be held to account in the usual way.[32] Also included in the report was a plea for whistleblowers to first use internal channels; external channels or the greater public should only be addressed if internal channels do not exist or have not functioned properly.[33] Moreover, the report correctly denoted how an effective whistleblower protection was directly relevant for the protection of the rights guaranteed under the European Convention on Human Rights.[34]

The report stated that "[w]histle-blowers are not traitors, but people with courage who prefer to take action against abuses they come across rather than taking the easy route and remaining silent. To pass this message across Europe will be the most important contribution this report can make."[35] Therefore, whistleblowing was an important value for the society in general. The discussion arose as to the level of reported misconduct, whether only criminal acts triggered the protection or if illegal or even immoral acts did too, or alternatively if only specific activities were worthy of protection. At the same time, whistleblowing would only include a non-self-interested complaint, where the whistleblowing person was only remotely affected by the reported incident, if at all.[36]

After having analysed several national acts addressing this issue, the report highlighted some aspects as best practices to be taken into account:[37] First, the focus of a filed report should not be restricted to corruption cases but extend to any kind of malpractice or illegal behaviour as long as it was in the public interest. Second, the whistleblower protection should apply to both the public and the private sector. Third, whistleblower protection should not end with a protection from the own employer. Fourth, whistleblower protection should most importantly focus on the protection of the whistleblower's identity. Fifth,

[29] Report on the protection of whistleblowers (2009), p. 1.

[30] Report on the protection of whistleblowers (2009), p. 1.

[31] Report on the protection of whistleblowers (2009), p. 21.

[32] Report on the protection of whistleblowers (2009), p. 21.

[33] Report on the protection of whistleblowers (2009), p. 4.

[34] Report on the protection of whistleblowers (2009), p. 19.

[35] Report on the protection of whistleblowers (2009), p. 6.

[36] Report on the protection of whistleblowers (2009), p. 9.

[37] Report on the protection of whistleblowers (2009), pp. 20–22.

a whistleblower need not file a report anonymously for it to be most effectively investigated. Sixth, the protection was only triggered by a report in good faith, unless it was of specific public interest. Seventh, any burden of proof should be ascertained in a whistleblower-friendly manner.

2.1.1.5 Resolution 1729 (2010) of the Parliamentary Assembly of the Council of Europe

Following Report 12006 (2009) on the protection of whistleblowers, the Parliamentary Assembly adopted a corresponding resolution in 2010. The Parliamentary Assembly of the Council of Europe is the parliamentary institution of Europe's oldest international organisation. It consists of delegations from 47 national parliaments and is Europe's biggest democratic assembly.[38] Currently it consists of 591 members. It is also known as Europe's "democratic conscience".[39] The Parliamentary Assembly has various advisory functions as a democratic forum,[40] amongst them the capacity to issue recommendations and resolutions.[41] According to Rule 25.1.b Rules of Procedure of the Assembly defines a resolution as a decision by the Assembly on a question of substance which the Assembly is empowered to put into effect, or an expression of view for which it alone is responsible.

Resolution 1729 of the Parliamentary Assembly of the Council of Europe from 2010 emphasised in its paragraph 1 that whistleblowers can make a crucial contribution in the fight against mismanagement and corruption. Therefore, according to paragraph 6.1.1 of the resolution, protection is needed for warnings given in good faith about unlawful actions, especially those of serious human rights violations that affect or threaten the life, health, freedom or similar interests of individuals.[42] The basis for the protection of the whistleblower is the requirement of good faith in the factual basis of the hint. The whistleblower is no longer protected if he or she knows that the allegations are false or he or she has no reasonable grounds for such an assumption, according to paragraph 6.2.4 of the resolution.

---

[38] Parliamentary Assembly, see: https://www.coe.int/en/web/portal/parlamentarische-versammlung#{%2214943690%22:[0]} (last accessed: 14.09.2024).

[39] Parliamentary Assembly, see: https://www.coe.int/en/web/portal/parlamentarische-versammlung#{%2214943690%22:[0]} (last accessed: 14.09.2024).

[40] See Art. 22 Statute of the Council of Europe.

[41] See Rule 25 Rules of Procedure of the Assembly of the Council of Europe.

[42] Para. 6.1.1 Resolution 1729 (2010): "the definition of protected disclosures shall include all bona fide warnings against various types of unlawful acts, including all serious human rights violations which affect or threaten the life, health, liberty and any other legitimate interests of individuals as subjects of public administration or taxpayers, or as shareholders, employees or customers of private companies".

2.1.1.6 Feasibility Study "The Protection of Whistleblowers" (2012) on Behalf of the European Committee on Legal Co-Operation of the Council of Europe

The European Committee on Legal Co-operation of the Council of Europe commissioned a study in March 2012 lead by Paul Stephenson, the former member of the Ministry of Justice of the United Kingdom and expert in the field of corruption prevention together with Michael Levi, Professor of Criminology at the University of Cardiff. The study aimed at assessing the feasibility of developing a legal instrument to protect employees who make disclosures in the public interest. After the study analysed the protection measures already in place at that time, it concluded that further, more effective protection of whistleblowers was desirable and listed core principles in its appendix. However, the study referred in its paragraph 4.18 to the EU whistleblower protection instruments which then were still in their development phase. As a recommendation, the study in paragraph 5.4 mainly referred to the aforementioned principles and also called for a comprehensive and not just sectoral whistleblower protection.

According to paragraph 5.6. of the study, only those reports on violations, which are made in good faith, should trigger any whistleblower protection. Good faith should be equated with "honesty" according to Principle 4 of the appendix to the study. Good faith should be implied unless there is evidence for the contrary. This is in contrast to Report 12006 (2009). Especially for internal reports, according to Principle 5 of the Appendix to the study, it would suffice if the whistleblower has sufficient convincing reasons for suspecting the alleged misconduct, even if there is no conclusive evidence. The filed reports do not need to refer to pure legal violations, but according to paragraph 5.6 and Principle 2 of the study's Appendix, gross mismanagement, gross waste of money, abuse of authority or a significant and concrete danger to public health or safety are also sufficient. The intention of the whistleblower is again crucial for protection, so that personal advantages or pure acts of revenge should not trigger protection for the whistleblower, under paragraph 5.15 of the study.

The process of reporting follows a tiered process. Initially, an internal report should be made. If this is not possible or not successful, a report can be made to external bodies. The study makes it clear that publication via public media is not equivalent to external whistleblowing. The study also emphasises the importance of the confidentiality of the whistleblower in paragraphs 5.28 et seq., which should only be restricted in exceptional cases if the whistleblower consents to the disclosure of their identity in an informed manner regarding the consequences, or if this was necessary to avert serious and imminent dangers to the public interest.

2.1.1.7 Recommendation CM/Rec(2014)7 of the Committee of Ministers of the Council of Europe

The recommendation of the Council of Europe's Committee of Ministers of 30 April 2014 is an elaborate work that included a commentary section, which defined or at least described in a more comprehensive manner, principles for an effective whistleblower protection. For the first time, it defined a whistleblower as "any person who reports or discloses information on a threat or harm to the public interest in the context of their work-based relationship, whether it be in the public or private sector".[43] It generally emphasized that the relevant normative framework should reflect a comprehensive approach to enable public interest disclosures, hence the focus was on those cases that affected the public interest, not merely an issue of a single entity.[44] The public interest may, however, concern not only legal violations but also gross mismanagement.[45] The recommendation clarified in paragraph 18 especially, that the person giving the hint had a right to having their identity kept confidential. However, this guarantee of trust should not be unconditional at this point. Paragraph 18 expressly emphasises that confidentiality only extends as far as the principles for a fair trial are maintained. Without this being described further, it most likely refers to the meaning of Art. 6 para. 1 European Charter of Human Rights: In the case of a mere defamation case of the reporting person, his or her identity is no longer worth protecting and the alleged perpetrator has a right to an effective defence against the whistleblower. The recommendation was intended to help member states enact national whistleblower protection laws and thus emphasised in the comments that protection applies if the hint by the whistleblower was given "honestly". Honest or good faith does not mean that the whistleblower has no other motives or is ultimately right with his hint. Rather, it means according to paragraph 37 that he does not report information that he or she knows to be false. This corresponds to the findings from Report 12006 (2009). Additionally, the Recommendation provided various details and references to already existing case law by the European Court of Human Rights. Therefore, for understanding the development of the whistleblower protection it is important to shed some light on this relevant case law.

---

[43] Appendix to Recommendation CM/Rec(Committee of Ministers of the Council of Europe)7, Definitions.

[44] Appendix to Recommendation CM/Rec(Committee of Ministers of the Council of Europe)7, Principles, paras. 7, 13.

[45] Appendix to Recommendation CM/Rec(Committee of Ministers of the Council of Europe)7, Explanatory memorandum, para. 2.

2.1.2 *Protection Under the Convention for the Protection of Human Rights and Fundamental Freedoms (ECHR)*

The European Charter of Human Rights (ECHR) does not have an explicit right to whistleblower protection in its text. Nevertheless, the European Court of Human Rights (ECtHR) has interpreted such a right into the ECHR. The ECtHR is the most important body to interpret the rights and freedoms enshrined in the ECHR, and most importantly to develop them further as a living instrument.[46] Its decisions are therefore of particular weight in the development of whistleblower protection under the ECHR.

The decisions of the ECtHR, which deal with the protection of whistleblowing under Art. 10 ECHR[47] as the right to freedom of expression, regularly concerned external disclosures in the public sector. The court established in the case *Guja against Moldova*[48] six core principles to determine whether an interference with the right to freedom of expression under Art. 10 ECHR was "necessary in a democratic society" and may be justifiable under Art. 10 para. 2 ECHR.[49] These principles were expressly confirmed in the cases *Heinisch against Germany*[50] and *Halet against Luxembourg.*[51]

The ECtHR has recognised that whistleblowers in the context of a private employer situation also are protected by freedom of speech according to Art. 10 ECHR. The court ruled that the right under Art. 10 ECHR is fundamentally applicable to any employer-employee relationship, regardless of whether this relationship is one of public law or private law.[52] The right to freedom of speech grants protection especially in relationships between private individuals and also between employers and employees.[53]

---

[46] See first in ECtHR Judg. of 25.4.1978 – 5856/72, Tyrer against the United Kingdom.

[47] Art. 10 para. 1 sentence 1 and 2 ECHR state that "[e]veryone has the right to freedom of expression. This right shall include freedom to hold opinions and to receive and impart information and ideas without interference by public authority and regardless of frontiers".

[48] ECtHR Judg. of 12.2.2008 – 14277/04, Guja against Moldova.

[49] According to Art. 10 para. 2 ECHR "The exercise of these freedoms, since it carries with it duties and responsibilities, may be subject to such formalities, conditions, restrictions or penalties as are prescribed by law and are necessary in a democratic society, in the interests of national security, territorial integrity or public safety, for the prevention of disorder or crime, for the protection of health or morals, for the protection of the reputation or rights of others, for preventing the disclosure of information received in confidence, or for maintaining the authority and impartiality of the judiciary."

[50] ECtHR Judg. of 21.7.2011 – 28274/08, Heinisch against Germany.

[51] ECtHR Judg. of 11.5.2021 – 21884/18, Halet against Luxembourg.

[52] ECtHR Judg. of 8.12.2010 – 28955/06, 28957/06, 28959/06, 28964/06, Palomo Sánchez and others against Spain, para. 59; ECtHR Judg. of 14.9.2009 – 29492/05, Kudeshkina against Russia, para. 85; ECtHR Judg. of 29.2.2000 – 39293/98, Fuentes Bobo against Spain, para. 38.

[53] ECtHR Judg. of 16.2.2021 – 23922/19, Gawlik against Liechtenstein, para. 47; ECtHR Judg. of 5.9.2017 – 61496/08, Barbulescu against Romania, para. 108; ECtHR Judg. of 21.6.2016 – 79972/

However, Art. 10 para. 2 ECHR itself stipulates that restrictions on the right to freedom of speech also are permissible, among other things, if they are provided for by law and necessary in a democratic society. The necessity can arise in particular for maintaining order or for the prevention of crimes, for protection of good reputation or the rights of others or to prevent the dissemination of confidential information. The Court ruled that "necessary" in the sense of Art. 10 para. 2 ECHR implies the existence of an urgent social need.[54]

The ECtHR has also emphasised that an employee under employment law has general duties of loyalty, restraint and discretion that need to be observed.[55] Such obligations do not suddenly become void in a whistleblower context.

The following list of cases will not cover all decisions made on whistleblower protection but rather only those that are of particular relevance for the later balancing between the data protection right to information and whistleblower protection.

2.1.2.1 Tillack Against Belgium, No. 20477/05, Judgment of 27 November 2007

This case[56] concerned a whistleblower scenario that touched upon the confidentiality of sources of the press and was based on the following facts: The complainant, a journalist, published articles about alleged irregularities at Eurostat and in the Office for Fraud Prevention of the European Commission (OLAF), apparently based on tips from an official within OLAF. When the internal investigation of OLAF could not uncover the identity of the official, it filed a complaint with the Belgian authorities for bribery against the complainant. Allegedly, the complainant had bribed a civil servant to disclose confidential information.

The ECtHR found that Belgium violated Art. 10 ECHR when the Belgian police searched the journalist's home and office and confiscated certain documents. The claim by OLAF that the official might have been bribed was based on "mere rumours." The court emphasised that the right of journalists to protect their sources is not a "mere privilege that can be granted or taken away on the lawfulness or

12, Soares against Portugal, para. 39; ECtHR Judg. of 26.2.2009 – 29492/05, Kudeshkina against Russia, para. 85; ECtHR Judg. of 12.2.2008 – 14277/04, Guja against Moldova, para. 52.

[54] ECtHR Judg. of 15.2.2005 – 68416/01, Steel and Morris against the United Kingdom, para. 94; ECtHR Judg. of 26.4.1979 – 6538/74, Sunday Times (No. 1) against the United Kingdom, para. 59; ECtHR Judg. of 7.12.1976 – 5493/72, Handyside against the United Kingdom, para. 48.

[55] ECtHR Judg. of 16.2.2021 – 23922/19, Gawlik against Liechtenstein, para. 65; ECtHR Judg. of 21.6.2016 – 79972/12, Soares against Portugal, para. 41; ECtHR Judg. of 19.1.2016 – 12138/08, Aurelian Opera against Romania, para. 59; ECtHR Judg. of 17.9.2015 – 14464/11, Langner against Germany, para. 43; ECtHR Judg. of 13.1.2015 – 79040/12, Rubins against Latvia, para. 78; ECtHR Judg. of 12.2.2008 – 14277/04, Guja against Moldova, para. 70; ECtHR Judg. of 21.7.2011 – 28274/08, Heinisch against Germany, para. 63; ECtHR Judg. of 14.9.2009 – 29492/05, Kudeshkina against Russia, para. 85.

[56] ECtHR Judg. of 27.11.2007 – 20477/05, Tillack against Belgium.

unlawfulness of their sources," but rather it is a fundamental component of press freedom.[57] They stated that the national discretionary power is limited by the interest of a democratic society in ensuring and maintaining a free press. However here, the public official was protected because he informed the press of irregularities, hence as a whistleblower, rather than a press informant. On the side of the public official giving note of the irregularities to the press was therefore protected in the role of the whistleblower rather than as a source of the press. It is uncertain what conclusion would have been reached if there had been actual evidence of bribery by the journalist.

2.1.2.2 Guja Against Moldova, No. 14277/04, Judgement of 12 February 2008

The case of Guja against Moldova[58] is considered a landmark decision on whistleblower protection. The criteria established by the court in this case are frequently referred to in subsequent cases by the ECtHR as well as other expert reports to highlight essential principles of effective whistleblower protection.[59]

The complainant was the head of the press department of the Prosecutor General's Office in Moldova. After proceedings against some police officers for mistreatment of suspects had been discontinued, the complainant forwarded two letters to the media, which indicated that the proceedings may have been discontinued for improper reasons. One of these letters came from a high-ranking official of the Parliament. The complainant was dismissed because the letters were considered confidential (although they were not marked as such) and because he did not consult his superiors before forwarding the letters to the press.

In this case, the court established six principles for when an interference with rights under Art. 10 ECHR was "necessary in a democratic society".[60]

First, there must be a public interest in the reported information. The court found that the actions or omissions of an authority in a democratic system must be subject to close scrutiny by both the legislative and judicial authorities as well as by the media and public opinion. The public's interest in the disclosure of certain information can be so great in some circumstances that it may even override a statutorily prescribed duty of confidentiality. A whistleblower may therefore be justified in actually breaking confidentiality.

Second, it is important whether the whistleblower had alternative channels for the disclosure. In principle, the whistleblower must primarily use internal reporting channels to enjoy protection.[61] Only if such channels do not exist or, if the channels exist but do not function, may the whistleblower use external channels.

---

[57] ECtHR Judg. of 27.11.2007 – 20477/05, Tillack against Belgium, para. 65.

[58] ECtHR Judg. of 12.2.2008 – 14277/04, Guja against Moldova.

[59] See only Report above, at 1.1.4.

[60] ECtHR Judg. of 12.2.2008 – 14277/04, Guja against Moldova, paras. 69 et seq.

[61] ECtHR Judg. of 12.2.2008 – 14277/04, Guja against Moldova, para. 73.

Third, the disclosed information must be authentic. The court reaffirmed that freedom of expression also carries duties and responsibilities. This means specifically that anyone who chooses to disclose information must carefully verify the correctness and reliability of the information under the circumstances.

Fourth, in contrast to the EU Whistleblower Protection Directive, the personal motives of the whistleblower are significant. The court stated that reports motivated by personal grievances, personal hostilities or the expectation of personal advantage, including financial gain, do not justify a particularly high level of protection. In fact, those personal objectives regularly abrogate the protective mechanisms.

Fifth, the damage that may have been caused to the employer must be taken into account, especially whether this damage outweighs the public interest. The public interest may not in any case and in all situations outweigh the damage caused by the whistleblower.

Sixth, the severity of the sanction imposed on the whistleblower and its consequences must be taken into account.

In the Guja case, the court ultimately decided that there was a violation of Art. 10 ECHR and that under these circumstances external reporting, "even to a newspaper", was justified.[62] At its core, the court justified its decision with the importance of the topics. The public had a legitimate interest in being informed about the mistreatments of subjects by the police, especially as such topics touched upon the foundations of the rule of law in a democratic state and thus fell within the framework of political debate. The report was made against the backdrop of international concern about the collapse of the separation of powers and the lack of independence of the judiciary in Moldova.

In the end, the court argued that neither the law nor the rules of procedure of the Attorney General's Office contained provisions on the reporting of irregularities by employees and there was no evidence to refute the applicant's argument, namely that the other channels (the top ranks of his office or parliament) represented actual alternatives.[63]

2.1.2.3 Heinisch Against Germany, No. 28274/08, Judgment of 21 July 2011

The applicant in this case[64] was a nurse who worked in a nursing home. She was dismissed after her management did not respond to her reports of serious deficiencies in patient care. In the end, she filed a criminal complaint for fraud against the management of the nursing home. The national courts in Germany confirmed her dismissal on the grounds that the criminal complaint was a disproportionate response to her employer's refusal to acknowledge deficiencies and that she had violated her duty of loyalty to her employer.

---

[62] ECtHR Judg. of 12.2.2008 – 14277/04, Guja against Moldova, para. 84.

[63] ECtHR Judg. of 12.2.2008 – 14277/04, Guja against Moldova, para. 83.

[64] ECtHR Judg. of 21.7.2011 – 28274/08, Heinisch against Germany.

The Court dealt extensively with the specifics of the employment law situation and recognised in its judgment that employees indeed have a duty of loyalty to their employer. It stated that before a disclosure, a hint had to be made to the supervisor or another competent authority, first. Only if using such channel was obviously not feasible, may the information then be made available to the public as a last resort.

The ECtHR then examined this case in accordance with the principles established in the Guja case. It concluded that Art. 10 ECHR had been violated and noted in particular that the applicant had not only raised the staff shortages with her superiors, but also had alerted the management to a possible criminal complaint through her lawyer. Under those circumstances, an external hint in the form of a criminal complaint was justified. The court found that an employer who fails to remedy an illegal practice brought to their attention by an employee can no longer expect loyalty from that employee.

Furthermore, the applicant acted in good faith, even if it can be assumed that improving her own working conditions was another underlying motive for her action. The court found that this was corroborated by the fact that the applicant—having concluded that external reporting was necessary—did not immediately turn to the media but reported the facts to law enforcement instead.

Ultimately, the public interest in information about deficiencies in institutional elderly care was so important, it outweighed the interest in protecting the reputation and interests of the company.

2.1.2.4 Bucur and Toma Against Romania, No. 40238/02, Judgment of 8 April 2013

The case of Bucur and Toma against Romania focused on the actions of Constantin Bucur, an employee of the Romanian Intelligence Service (SRI), who disclosed classified information regarding illegal wiretapping activities conducted by the SRI. Mr. Bucur, who worked in the department responsible for monitoring and recording telephone communications, discovered several irregularities, including the unauthorized surveillance of journalists, politicians, and businessmen. Despite reporting these issues to his superiors, no action was taken. Consequently, Bucur decided to hold a press conference where he revealed the illegal activities and presented audio tapes as evidence.

Following the press conference, Bucur was prosecuted with several charges and convicted for disclosing classified information, theft of the audio tapes, and illegal wiretapping. He was sentenced to two years of imprisonment, which was ultimately suspended. The case also involved Mircea Toma, a journalist whose communications were intercepted, and his daughter, Sorana Toma, whose private conversations were recorded.

The ECtHR found that the charging and conviction Mr. Bucur due to his whistleblowing actions interfered with the right to freedom of expression under Art. 10 ECHR. The court emphasized the criteria that it stipulated in the Guja case, previously.[65] It especially highlighted that an officer working for the state bears a special loyalty obligation towards his or her employer, in particular when handling highly confidential information, and that a public disclosure of the information may only be justified under exceptional circumstances. Further relevant criteria are the authenticity of the information in question, the public interest in the information, the bona fide of the whistleblower, and the resultant damages. In the end, the court concluded that there was a violation of Art. 10 ECHR because Mr. Bucur, believing in the exceptional wrongdoing of the agency, had no other option than to go public and make a statement to the press.

2.1.2.5 Gawlik Against Liechtenstein, No. 23922/19, Judgment of 16 February 2021

In the case of Gawlik against Liechtenstein[66] the applicant Dr. Lothar Gawlik, deputy chief physician of the Liechtenstein State Hospital, reported that the hospital's chief physician had been involved in active euthanasia. He filed a complaint for mercy killing with the responsible public prosecutor's office, after he had unsuccessfully appealed to the president of the hospital's audit committee. After internal investigations, the suspicion was dispelled. According to the investigation results, the patients had been treated according to the applicable international World Health Organization (WHO) standards. Therefore, the suspicion of active euthanasia was unfounded. Only one expert interpreted the suspicion as "comprehensible".[67]

As a result, Dr. Gawlik was extraordinarily dismissed. After exhausting domestic legal remedies and filing an individual complaint to the ECtHR, the court dealt with the case. The Court anchored its decision in Art. 10 ECHR, the right to freedom of expression. Ultimately, the ECtHR found that the dismissal had been justified. The court examined the Guja and Heinisch criteria, namely: public interest in the information; the authenticity of the information; opportunities to report grievances to superiors or other responsible bodies first; any damage to the employer; the motives of the whistleblower; and the severity and consequences of the imposed sanction.[68]

According to the ECtHR's judgement, the complainant had a significant public interest in the information, as it was a possible case of active euthanasia. Also, he initially reported the suspicion to the audit committee. His motives were considered to be upright by the court. Ultimately, however, the court lacked the authenticity of the information. Experts attested to obvious unfoundedness. Had Dr. Gawlik investigated the circumstances more thoroughly, by consulting patients' paper

[65] ECtHR Judg. of 8.1.2013 – 40238/02, Bucur and Roma against Romania, para. 93.

[66] ECtHR Judg. of 16.2.2021 – 23922/19, Gawlik against Liechtenstein.

[67] ECtHR Judg. of 16.2.2021 – 23922/19, Gawlik against Liechtenstein, para. 53.

[68] ECtHR Judg. of 16.2.2021 – 23922/19, Gawlik against Liechtenstein, para. 64 ff.

files in addition to the electronic files, he would have notices his misjudgement. Therefore, the dismissal was justified.

This case is noteworthy because it established concrete obligations for the whistleblower. Although it did not occur in the context of a data protection right to information, it dealt with the inaccuracy of the filed information. Overall, a basic duty to investigate should be permissible. Especially with such severe accusations, hasty hints can easily have massive disadvantages for the accused. The more serious the accusation, the greater the duty to investigate before filing a report.

2.1.2.6 Halet Against Luxembourg, No. 21884/18, Judgements of 11 May 2021 and 14 February 2023

The complainant in this case,[69] Raphaël Halet was employed by the accountancy firm PricewaterhouseCoopers (PwC) which offers, in particular, auditing, tax consulting, and corporate management services.

The complainant came into contact with 14 tax returns of international companies in the course of his work at PwC. He passed these on to journalists in violation of both tax secrecy and the duty of loyalty under employment law. The journalist subsequently produced international and generally accessible reports on these corporate tax returns (the so-called "Luxleaks" affair).[70] The published information shed light on a practice of extremely advantageous tax agreements over a period from 2002 to 2012 between the Luxembourg tax authorities and PwC, the latter acting on behalf of multinational companies. The tax practices triggered a general debate but were completely legal under Luxembourg law and accordingly, did not violate any national law.

The complainant was criminally convicted because the courts did not see him as a protected whistleblower and did not accept his motivation as a justification for his actions. However, the other person involved in the revelations, Antoine Deltour, was acquitted on the grounds that he had indeed acted as a whistleblower and therefore enjoyed corresponding protection. The courts justified the distinction between the two men by pointing out that Mr. Deltour first brought the information to light whereas Mr. Halet only provided further information on the already known case. Mr. Halet was fined 1,000 EUR for violation of trade secrets. The moderate penalty was justified by the courts through the relevance of the violated public interest and the fact that the denounced behaviour was not illegal under national law.

The third Chamber of the ECtHR also decided against Mr. Halet.[71] Notably, the Court emphasised that Art. 10 ECHR implies a positive obligation of the state to provide effective protection for whistleblowers in the employment context. In this

[69] ECtHR Judg. of 11.5.2021 – 21884/18, Halet against Luxembourg.

[70] Meyer (2023), p. 261.

[71] ECtHR Judg. of 11.5.2021 – 21884/18, Halet against Luxembourg.

regard it prominently referred to the principles of Recommendation CM/Rec(2014) 7 of the Committee of Ministers of the Council of Europe of 30 April 2014 as well as to Resolution 1729 of 2010 of the Parliamentary Assembly of the Council of Europe.[72] When applying the standards, it found that the criminal proceedings against Mr. Halet as well as his conviction were actually in line with the Court's standards under Art. 10 ECHR and the right to freedom of expression. The Court therefore applied the previously established Guja criteria. It concluded that the disclosures had been of public interest and that the information Mr. Halet disclosed had been true. Furthermore, it confirmed that the engagement with the media and using public channels was the only real chance to actually inform the public about the issues. Internal reporting mechanisms had not been effective. Moreover, the whistleblower had been of good faith so no other motives had steered his decision to inform the public.

However, the third Chamber, was of the opinion that the balance between the public interest in being informed about the wrongdoing and the harm caused to the employer did not clearly speak in favour of the complainant, Mr. Halet. The employer, PwC enjoyed great trust by their clients and the disclosed information had the potential of long lasting harm to the firm's reputation by way of diminishing its clients' trust in it and in its internal security mechanisms, which outweighed the general public's interest in being made aware of the questionable, though not illegal, practices. The third Chamber was convinced that the firm did suffer harm in the short term. At the same time no long-term harm could be found. Although the damage for the firm did not last for a long period of time, the Third Chamber found that the harm suffered by PwC outweighed the interest of Mr. Halet's disclosures.

Furthermore, the third Chamber opined that Mr. Halet's penalty as a consequence of his actions, a fine of 1,000 Euros, was relatively mild and did not contribute to a chilling effect on others to come forward in other situations. After all, according to the third Chamber, the whistleblower, Mr. Halet, had no right to publicly address the issues through the media and exceed his right to freedom of expression under Art. 10 ECHR.

This decision taken by the majority of judges was then criticized by four judges in a joint dissenting opinion.[73] This opinion vastly contested the ruling on the role of public interest as it allegedly reduced legal certainty when applying the Guja criteria. It pointed out that the existing categories[74] of conduct on an employer's part, namely "unlawful acts, practices or conduct in the workplace" and "acts, practices or conduct which, although legal, are reprehensible" were amended by a new third category. This new category turns out to be "certain information that concerns the functioning of public authorities in a democratic society and sparks a public debate, giving rise to controversy likely to create a legitimate interest on the public's part in having

[72] ECtHR Judg. of 11.5.2021 – 21884/18, Halet against Luxembourg, para. 39.

[73] Joint Dissenting Opinion of Judges Ravarani, Mourou-Vikström, Chanturia, and Sabato to ECtHR Judg. of 11.5.2021 – 21884/18, Halet against Luxembourg.

[74] ECtHR Judg. of 14.2.2023 – 21884/18, Halet against Luxembourg, para. 137.

knowledge of the information in order to reach an informed opinion as to whether or not it reveals harm to the public interest".[75] The judges of the dissenting opinion argued that such a category would not be necessary to solve the case of Mr. Halet, that the references made to another case when establishing the third category ignores the fundamental differences of that other case, and finally that the new criterion would be extremely vague and cause legal uncertainty.

The case was finally decided by the ECtHR's Grand Chamber.[76] In its decision it confirmed the Guja criteria, specified and consolidated its case law, but at the same time expanded the protection area for whistleblowers. It is therefore the second large landmark decision after the Guja case.[77] The Grand Chamber explained that, first, the Guja criteria—although remaining the correct guidance in such cases—is not to be taken as having a strict hierarchy or a specific order in which the criteria must be applied. The rationale behind the criteria is to confirm whether a fair balance has been struck between the public interest and the detrimental effects of the disclosure. For example, the fact that there was already a public debate about tax practices in place in Luxembourg did not reduce the importance of the published information by Mr. Halet as he still published the information to make known the circumstances of the situation he discovered.[78] Moreover, the Grand Chamber found that the third Chamber did not conduct a sufficiently thorough examination on the detrimental effects for the employer and that the alleged damage done to the image of PwC and the loss of clients' confidence was not demonstrated to a necessary degree.

As to Mr. Halet's sanction, the Grand Chamber found that the detriment amounted to 15,000 Euros of non-pecuniary damage and 40,000 Euros of lost profit and Mr. Halet also spent over ten years in litigation which had negative reputational consequences. Therefore, a compensation may not be fully outweighing all of his losses. In the end, the Grand Chamber found a violation of the right to freedom of expression under Art. 10 ECHR and of the available whistleblower protection.

2.1.2.7 Interim Conclusions

The Court regularly applied the whistleblower protection to both private[79] and public[80] employees. In most of the cases, the Court reiterated the importance of the

[75] ECtHR Judg. of 14.2.2023 – 21884/18, Halet against Luxembourg, para. 138.

[76] ECtHR Judg. of 14.2.2023 – 21884/18, Halet against Luxembourg.

[77] Cf. also Scheu (2024), p. 61; Andreadakis and Kafteranis (Andreadakis and Kafteranis).

[78] ECtHR Judg. of 14.2.2023 – 21884/18, Halet against Luxembourg, paras 175 et seq.

[79] ECtHR Judg. of 18.10.2011 – 10247/09, Sosinowska against Poland; ECtHR Judg. of 15.11.2012 – 53579/09 and 53582/09, Bargao and Domingos Correia against Portugal; ECtHR Judg. of 21.7.2011 – 28274/08, Heinisch against Germany; ECtHR Judg. of 12.10.2010 – 49001/07, Bathellier against France; ECtHR Judg. of 30.9.2010 – 28369/07, Balenovic against Croatia.

[80] ECtHR Judg. of 8.1.2013 – 40238/02, Bucur and Toma against Romania; ECtHR Judg. of 26.2.2009 – 29492/05, Kudeshkina against Russia.

Guja criteria. These criteria are six in total, namely (1) priority of internal reporting channels over external reporting to the press, (2) the public interest of the disclosed information, (3) the authenticity of the disclosed information reasonably verified by the whistleblower, (4) the detriment to the employer, (5) the good faith of the whistleblower, and (6) the severity of the sanction by the employer.[81]

The Court also applied the Guja criteria, in a more general sense, in cases other than typical whistleblower cases. It pointed out in Halet against Luxembourg that the legal concept of the whistleblower is not yet clearly defined. Although there have been attempts of more concise elaboration or definitions such as in the Recommendation CM/Rec(2014)7 of the Committee of Ministers of the Council of Europe, a concise legal definition under the ECHR has not yet been carved out. So far, the Court has always refrained from an abstract and general definition. Therefore, the circumstances of each individual case must be considered as well as the context in which the case occurred. In individual cases, it can even happen that the Court denies the status of a whistleblower, yet still applies the Guja criteria to the non-whistleblower.[82]

The caselaw of the ECtHR shows that the Guja case, including its established criteria, are part of the landmark rules for assessing the legality of whistleblowing. Even in another core decision, the Halet case, the Court once again referred to the Guja criteria. The important references can be found both in the ruling of the third Chamber as well as the ruling of the Grand Chamber. What is not entirely clear and consistent in the various decisions, though, is the preponderance of certain of the criteria over others. Against the backdrop of those decisions, the ECtHR followed a rather ad hoc balancing approach as opposed to a systematic application of the said criteria.[83]

The second key case is the Halet case. In that case, the Court was of the opinion that the complainant was allowed to give the information to the journalists. According to the court, when applying and evaluating a specific case, it is important not to view the criteria as equal boxes to be checked. The reporting of hints does not have to follow a strict hierarchy. This means a whistleblower does not necessarily have to first turn to an internal reporting office. Interestingly in the Halet case, the complainant was allowed to give the information directly to the journalists because the practised "tax optimisation tricks" did not violate Luxembourg laws at all. Therefore, in the opinion of the Court, neither the employer nor the official reporting offices were able to provide legal remedy. This criterion has also been carefully addressed in other decisions such as Matuz against Hungary, but the preponderance of the internal channels has repeatedly

[81] ECtHR Judg. of 12.2.2008 – 14277/04, Guja against Moldova.

[82] Cf. ECtHR Judg. of 13.1.2015 – 79040/12, Rubins against Latvia; ECtHR Judg. of 19.1.2016 – 12138/08, Aurelian Opera against Romania.

[83] Scheu (2024), p. 61.

been confirmed in the Court's practice.[84] In that regard, the Court consulted with and referred to the Whistleblower Protection Directive of the European Union which does not prefer the internal over the external channels. Hence the ECtHR practice here is different from EU law.

At the same time, in the Halet case, the accuracy and authenticity of the information provided was never questioned but simply presumed throughout the entire process. Additionally, the complainant did not act out of greed for profit or simply to harm his employer, hence his disclosure was justified as being made in good faith. This criterion has been consistently applied at least when other motives such as personal grievances or personal antagonism were particularly dominant. This again is an aspect where the EU's legal protection and the Whistleblower Protection Directive differ from the ECtHR's jurisprudence.

The ECtHR also considered the damage to the employer or third parties. In particular, it made statements on aspects such as good reputation, confidentiality obligations, and tax, professional and trade secrets. Also, internal information must be adequately protected against data leaks. In this regard, the Court came to the conclusion that the damage incurred by the complainant's employer could not be assessed solely in terms of the possible financial implications of the contested disclosure. It accepted that PwC had suffered some reputational damage. Apparently, however, a long-term damage could not be proven.

In assessing the severity of the sanction, however, the court applied a rather strict standard. It warned emphatically against a deterrent, paralysing effect, which could discourage well-intentioned whistleblowers from reporting. Therefore, the fine of 1,000 EUR was already considered too high.

To some extent, the Court went beyond the criteria of its previous case law, especially regarding the assessment of an existing public interest and the overall balancing of interests. Until then, whistleblower protection in terms of the public interest was only related to reports of illegal behaviour or unlawful conditions.[85] The Court emphasised in Halet however, that even legal behaviour can lead to a publication of the information being contrary to confidentiality interests. The balance must be based on the relevance for the affected society. In this case, the reported information was considered alarming or scandalous and provided new insights. The information about the tax practices of multinational companies, for example, those whose tax returns the complainant later published, undoubtedly contributed to a general debate about tax evasion, transparency, fairness and tax justice.

As a result, the Court struck an overall balance of the involved interests. However, it established a relative weight of the disclosed information in view of their nature and the extent of the risk associated with their disclosure. Given the

[84] ECtHR Judg. of 21.10.2014 – 73571/10, Matuz against Hungary.

[85] ECtHR Judg. of 12.2.2008 – 14277/04, Guja against Moldova, para. 72; ECtHR Judg. of 21.7.2011 – 28274/08, Heinisch against Germany, para. 63; ECtHR Judg. of 19.1.2016 – 12138/08, Aurelian Opera against Romania, para. 71.

importance of the public debate about the tax practices of multinational companies, at both the national and the European levels, to which the information disclosed by Mr. Halet had made a significant contribution, the Court came to the conclusion that the disclosure of this information outweighed all adverse effects.

The ECtHR emphasised that in that case it was not only about the disclosure of information by the complainant per se, but also about the unlawful theft of the data carrier with the information and, that in this context, the public interest in preventing and punishing theft also had to be considered. It pointed out that the complainant was not only bound by the employee's duty of loyalty and confidentiality towards his employer but also by professional secrecy, which applied in the specific area of the activities carried out by PwC and to which he was legally bound in the exercise of his professional activity. These aspects were seen by the lower courts as a weighty reason against the protection of the complainant. The upper court, however, criticised the lack of depth in the reasoning in relation to the specific situation.

After all, various legal sources agree on the principles, namely, that whistleblowers who report an actual violation of certain regulations generally enjoy protection. However, the legal sources are unclear on details, such as the meaning of good faith ("sufficient reasons", "reasonable reasons", "honesty"). Also, there is no direct consensus on the meaning of the whistleblower's disposition or the importance of the reported violation. The assessment of this question in the employment law context appears even more complicated, where further possible conflicting rights must be considered.

Before assessing the mentioned criteria, another source for the protection of whistleblowers should be taken into consideration, namely the EU Whistleblower Directive (**see under 2.**).

2.2 Protection of Whistleblowers According to Directive (EU) 2019/1937 (Whistleblower Protection Directive)

The European Parliament and the Council of the European Union adopted EU Directive 2019/1937, on 7 October 2019, for the protection of persons working for a public or private organisation or that are in contact with such an organisation. The directive came into force on 16 December 2019. For the Member States of the European Union, it provided a two-year transition period until 17 December 2021 to implement the contents of the directive into domestic law. Virginie Rozière, former member of the EU Parliament and then rapporteur on the whistleblower directive, cited the incidents around LuxLeaks or the Panama Papers as key triggers.[86] The EU legislator considered it particularly important that informants

[86] European Parliament, Press Release (European Parliament).

who expose misconduct in a company are protected from reprisals by their employers and enjoy extensive confidentiality.

The Whistleblower Protection Directive differs from the conventional protection in its scope. First, the Directive is partly based on a human rights foundation. Recital 14 of the Directive names respect for privacy and the protection of personal data in the sense of Art. 7 and 8 EU Charter of Fundamental Rights as the protective scope of the Directive. However, the Directive also has other aims. It became clear in the past, that whistleblowing was a complex undertaking. It tackled issues such as the fight against corruption, the prevention of crimes in more general, public procurement and the functioning of EU competition law, product safety and consumer protection, as well as environmental protection and public health.[87] The EU has a greater variety of competences than the Council of Europe and the human rights perspective. Consequently, the Directive is different in certain ways. It only applies to very specific violations and refers in Art. 3 Whistleblower Protection Directive in conjunction with Annex Part 2 to numerous special regulations with priority over the more general scope of the directive. At the same time, conventional protection of whistleblowers depends on extensive, individual case-by-case examinations and therefore is less clearly defined.[88] This may be due to the fact that the Directive primarily focuses on effective law enforcement and does not follow human rights mandates.[89] The Directive actually addresses its relationship to the conventional protection of whistleblowing. Recital 31 of the Directive mentions the situation of a particular harm or threat to the public interest and the importance of the right to freedom of expression and to impart and receive information. It also says "*Accordingly, this Directive draws upon the case law of the European Court of Human Rights (ECHR) on the right to freedom of expression, and the principles developed on this basis by the Council of Europe in its Recommendation on the Protection of Whistleblowers adopted by its Committee of Ministers on 30 April 2014.*" Recital 33 also refers to the relationship between the Directive and the conventional human rights protection. When addressing the reporting mechanisms and the question whether the whistleblower should be able to choose freely between internal or external channels, the recital reads: "*Moreover, it is necessary to protect public disclosures, taking into account democratic principles such as transparency and accountability, and fundamental rights such as freedom of expression and the freedom and pluralism of the media, whilst balancing the interest of employers to manage their organisations and to protect their interests, on the one hand, with the interest of the public to be protected from harm, on the other, in line with the criteria developed in the case law of the ECHR.*" However, the exact nuances of the several obligations in question are not entirely clarified by these references. To what extent these criteria

[87] Scheu (2024), p. 59.

[88] Meyer (2023), p. 276.

[89] Meyer (2023), p. 276.

should be directly considered in the balance between whistleblower-protection-interest and information-interest on the employer's part need to be clarified.

2.2.1 Personal Scope of the Whistleblower Protection Directive

The personal scope of the Whistleblower Protection Directive is generally broad. Art. 4 para. 1 of the Whistleblower Protection Directive states that it applies to persons who are active in the private or public sector and have obtained information about certain legal violations listed in the Directive in a professional context. The scope also extends far in terms of time. According to Art. 4 para. 2 of the Whistleblower Protection Directive, those whistleblowers also are protected who report or disclose information about violations of which they became aware during a now terminated employment relationship. According to Art. 4 para. 3 of the Whistleblower Protection Directive, even those persons are protected whose employment relationship has not yet begun and who, during the recruitment process or other pre-contractual negotiations, have obtained information about violations. In addition, the protection applies to other persons, including those who convey a hint, colleagues who could also suffer reprisals, and others listed in Art. 4 para. 4 of the Whistleblower Protection Directive. Recital 37 sentence 1 of the Whistleblower Protection Directive puts it to the point: Effective enforcement of EU law requires that as broad a range of groups of persons as possible should be protected. It is irrelevant whether they are EU citizens or third-country nationals. The decisive factor is that they, due to their professional activity, regardless of the nature of this activity and whether it is remunerated, have privileged access to information about violations and their reporting is in the public interest. Although the recitals are not part of the operational part of the directive, they can give important guidance on the interpretation of the actual provisions of the directive.

2.2.2 Material Scope of the Whistleblower Protection Directive

In terms of content, according to Art. 2 the Whistleblower Protection Directive initially covers the legal areas explicitly listed in its para. 2. These include, for example, product safety and product conformity (Art. 2 para. 1. a) iii) Whistleblower Protection Directive), traffic safety (Art. 2 para. 1. a) iv) Whistleblower Protection Directive) or environmental protection (Art. 2 para. 1. a) v) Whistleblower Protection Directive).

According to Recital 48 sentence 2 of the Whistleblower Protection Directive, all companies with 50 or more employees who are under the obligation to collect value added tax (VAT) in their respective countries, regardless of the nature of their activities, should set up internal reporting channels for persons, who may wish to come forward with information.

2.2.3 *Conditions for the Protection of Whistleblowers*

Art. 6 Whistleblower Protection Directive is of particular importance for the protection of whistleblowers. Generally, the scope of the directive is very broadly formulated because a whistleblower should be protected as much as possible. Nevertheless, Art. 6 prescribes that the reported information must meet procedural and qualitative requirements. To wit, a whistleblower must adhere to the existing reporting processes, Art. 6 para. 1. b) Whistleblower Protection Directive. This means, for example, he must generally use the existing internal reporting channels, Art. 7 para. 1 Whistleblower Protection Directive. Also, the whistleblower must have sufficient reason to believe that the reported information about the respective violations were true at the time of reporting and that this information fell within the scope of this directive, Art. 6 para. 1. a) Whistleblower Protection Directive.

2.2.4 *The Guja/Halet Criteria Under the Whistleblower Protection Directive*

The Guja criteria can be found partially in the Whistleblower Protection Directive as well, yet with certain differences.[90]

2.2.4.1 Priority of Internal Reporting Channels Over External Reporting Channels

The first difference between the Whistleblower Protection Directive and the caselaw of the ECtHR (Guja) is the priority of internal reporting channels over external ones. Whereas the whistleblower protection deriving from the ECHR requires the whistleblower to first use internal channels and only use external channels or directly the public media as a last resort, the Whistleblower Protection Directive sees those channels as equal and gives the whistleblower the right to choose the best way to address their complaint. Recital 33 of the Directive acknowledges that persons normally feel more at ease with internal reporting; "the reporting person should be able to choose the most appropriate reporting channel depending on the individual circumstances of the case". Yet interestingly, Recital 33 equally addresses the existing caselaw of the ECtHR stating that "it is necessary to protect public disclosures, taking into account democratic principles such as transparency and accountability, and fundamental rights such as freedom of expression and the freedom and pluralism of the media, whilst balancing the interest of employers to manage their organizations and to

[90] On the specifications of the Whistleblower Protection Directive in an international context in general: Lewis (2020), p. 1 et seq.

protect their interests, on the one hand, with the interest of the public to be protected from harm, on the other, in line with the criteria developed in the case law of the ECHR".

In the end, the Whistleblower Protection Directive is not solely concerned with the relationship between an employer and an employee, hence the loyalty towards the employer is not a decisive factor, but it may well be recognized in this context.[91] Some authors argue that loyalty towards the employer and whistleblower are not in conflict with one another.[92] Informing about irregularities may go hand in hand with one's loyalty towards the employer. It is supposed to be comparable to a friend having a drug problem and in need of external help. Moreover, some authors even see an obligation to blow the whistle.[93] Yet, from a labour law point of view—although the scope of the Whistleblower Protection Directive is broader also due to a lack of labour law competences[94]—there are loyalty obligations on the side of the employee towards the employer. Taking this into consideration, one should interpret the Directive accordingly, and generally claim a first attempt for an internal report. As such, Art. 7 para. 2 of the Directive states that "Member States shall encourage reporting through internal reporting channels before reporting through external reporting channels, where the breach can be addressed effectively internally and where the reporting person considers that there is no risk of retaliation".

2.2.4.2 Public Interest of the Disclosed Information

The exact dominance of this criterion is not fundamental to any sort of reporting. In Art. 15 para. 1. b) i) Whistleblower Protection Directive requires that the person making use of a public reporting must have reasonable grounds to believe that the reported breach may constitute an imminent or manifest danger to the public interest. The public interest is also mentioned in several Recitals such as Recitals 42, 48, and 84. Overall, in situations of public disclosures, the most weight would be given to the criterion of the public interest.

2.2.4.3 Authenticity of the Disclosed Information Reasonably Verified by the Whistleblower

Recital 32 reads that "reporting persons should have reasonable grounds to believe, in light of the circumstances and the information available to them at the time of reporting, that the matters reported by them are true". It furthermore points out that "requirement is an essential safeguard against malicious and frivolous or abusive

[91] Kobron-Gasiorowska (2022), p. 199; in more general: Varelius (2008), p. 263 et seq.

[92] Larmer (2022), p. 128.

[93] Vandekerckhove, Commers (Vandekerckhove and Commers 2004), p. 225 et seq.

[94] Cf. to the basis of the Whistleblower Protection Directive: Kafteranis (2021), p. 65 et seq.

reports as it ensures that those who, at the time of the reporting, deliberately and knowingly reported wrong or misleading information do not enjoy protection. At the same time, the requirement ensures that protection is not lost where the reporting person reported inaccurate information on breaches by honest mistake". This is also an important factor for the protection of the confidentiality of a whistleblower's identity under Art. 6 para. 1. a) Whistleblower Protection Directive.

2.2.4.4 Detriment to the Employer

From the Guja/Halet criteria, the aspect of the detriment or harm to the employer is not explicitly mentioned in the Directive; nor is there anything in this regard in the Recitals.

2.2.4.5 Good Faith of the Whistleblower

The criterion of bona fide or good faith of the whistleblower is at the core of the jurisprudence of the ECtHR and is absolutely essential to whistleblower protection. For the Court, a whistleblower acting with personal grievances or who is motivated by frustration as a result of not getting promoted is not worthy of a whistleblower's protection. Such requirement is not foreseen in the Whistleblower Protection Directive. Yet, while the ECtHR takes this aspect as a motivational criterion for sorting out certain persons, the Whistleblower Protection Directive uses another aspect for that matter. Thus, Recital 32 reads that "reporting persons should have reasonable grounds to believe, in light of the circumstances and the information available to them at the time of reporting, that the matters reported by them are true", and that such requirement "is an essential safeguard against malicious and frivolous or abusive reports as it ensures that those who, at the time of the reporting, deliberately and knowingly reported wrong or misleading information do not enjoy protection". People who know exactly that their reported information is false or deliberately report false or even misleading information, are not in need of protection (Recital 32 Whistleblower Protection Directive). Apart from that, the whistleblower may follow further ulterior motives.

The most common case in practice is probably the one in which the whistleblower has not obtained any evidence for his suspicion, but is convinced of the existence of a violation based on the facts readily available to him. According to Recital 32 Whistleblower Protection Directive, protection even applies in the case that the whistleblower has reported inaccurate information, as long as he was acting in good faith with regard to this. Accordingly, those people should also be in need of protection who are acting in good faith not with regard to the information itself, but to the scope of the Directive (Recital 32 Whistleblower Protection Directive).

According to the legislative intent of the Whistleblower Protection Directive, the intention of the whistleblower is irrelevant as long as the information they are reporting is true or they are acting in good faith and comply with the other requirements. So technically, it is possible that a whistleblower wants to take revenge on an unpopular colleague or a disturbing superior and therefore—but correctly—files a report. The motive of personal revenge could, strictly speaking, even be his primary goal without him being concerned about correcting an illegal action at all. Nevertheless, he could initially fall within the scope of the Directive as long as the information he reports is true (Recital 32 Whistleblower Protection Directive).

2.2.4.6 Severity of the Sanction

In this context, the whistleblower is protected against retaliations and other detriments by the employer.[95] Just as in the context of the whistleblower protection of the Council of Europe, this criterion is somewhat subsidiary.

2.2.4.7 Summary

Generally, it is understood that the Whistleblower Protection Directive diverges somewhat from the protection offered through the jurisprudence of the ECtHR.[96] The ECtHR whistleblower protection focuses exclusively on the human rights aspects, trying to balance both the whistleblowers' interests and the employers' interests based on their respective human rights and business interests. The EU protection of whistleblowers, though, encompasses a broader ranger of interests. The EU law essentially focuses on the objective value of the reporting, whereas the efficiency of the fight against corruption, fraud, and other illegal activities is independent from the personal motivation of the whistleblower. This is ultimately legitimate as the concept and theories of whistleblowing are more diverse than unique.[97] Moreover, the Whistleblower Protection Directive is not concerned only with the protection of workers or employees, but also it establishes whistleblowing as a general tool for reporting irregularities.[98]

2.2.5 *Confidentiality of the Whistleblower's Identity*

The confidentiality of the whistleblower's identity is one of the core elements of whistleblower protection in the Whistleblower Protection Directive. This is not

[95] Article 3 para. 4, Recital 44 Whistleblower Protection Directive.

[96] Scheu (2024), p. 64.

[97] Cf. e.g. on the theories of whistleblowing: Kobron-Gasiorowska (2022), p. 193.

[98] Kobron-Gasiorowska (2022), p. 196.

surprising at first, because a whistleblower can easily end up in the crossfire of other participants. If they report a work colleague and suspects him or her of an illegal act, this will not please the accused. If the reported act is knowingly tolerated or even supported among colleagues, then the only one standing out is the whistleblower; hence, the risk of reprisals against the whistleblower easily can increase. Largely, in order for the whistleblower to be protected, their identity must be protected. Recital 82 para. 1. Whistleblower Protection Directive also states that the protection of the identity of the whistleblower during the reporting process and the investigations triggered by it is an essential precautionary measure against reprisals.

When establishing internal reporting channels, a company generally has the choice of which ones to establish. While a company enjoys a margin of assessment, it is nevertheless the highest command to maintain the confidentiality of the whistleblower's identity (Recital 53). Recital 3 Whistleblower Protection Directive prescribes that "it is necessary to enhance enforcement by introducing effective, confidential and secure reporting channels". At the same time, the Directive is not aimed at affecting the protection of confidentiality of communications between lawyers and their clients ('legal professional privilege').[99] Art. 9 para. 1. a) Whistleblower Protection Directive stipulates that both internal reports and follow-up measures must be designed, set up and operated in such a way that the confidentiality of the whistleblower's identity is maintained. The high value of the confidentiality of the whistleblower's identity applies not only to internal reports, but also to external reporting channels according to Art. 12 para. 1. a) Whistleblower Protection Directive. The employers must ensure the integrity and confidentiality of the information if they want to be considered independent and autonomous.

Against the background of confidentiality, information about the identity of the whistleblower may only be disclosed with the express consent of the whistleblower according to Art. 16 para. 1. first sentence Whistleblower Protection Directive. This also applies to information that does not contain the identity of the whistleblower itself but, from which, the identity can be directly or indirectly derived, according to Art. 16 para. 1. second sentence Whistleblower Protection Directive. Exceptions to confidentiality apply exclusively when this is a necessary and proportionate obligation in the context of official measures or court proceedings, Art. 16 para. 2 Whistleblower Protection Directive. While protecting the whistleblower, the Directive also explicitly dictates that the accused person's rights to defend themselves equally must be maintained; the accused person must be able to effectively defend themselves against defamation or other insults or slander. This is only sufficiently possible if the accused person knows who they have to proceed against, i.e. the whistleblower.

A breach of the duty of confidentiality is ultimately punishable by a fine, Art. 23 para. 1. d) Whistleblower Protection Directive. An exact amount is not mentioned

[99] Recital 26 Whistleblower Protection Directive.

in the Whistleblower Protection Directive. The sanction is to be determined by the national legislator in the context of the implementation of the Whistleblower Protection Directive into national law. However, the sanctions must be effective, proportionate and dissuasive.[100]

2.3 Conclusion

The Whistleblower Protection Directive offers protection for the whistleblower who properly reports certain violations from the disclosure of their identity. In terms of time, the Whistleblower Protection Directive goes far, in terms of content it is limited to specifically named violations. After all, the Directive only offers minimum harmonization standards.[101]

The wording of the EU Whistleblower Protection Directive is noteworthy as it does not differ from Resolution 1729 of the Parliamentary Assembly of the Council of Europe from 2010. While the resolution mentions "reasonable grounds", the Whistleblower Protection Directive also speaks of "reasonable grounds", but that those reasonable grounds require "sufficient evidence". The Whistleblower Protection Directive does not explicitly mention "good faith", yet it is legitimate to summarize this aspect as good faith. According to the Resolution, if a person enjoys the protection of a good faith whistleblower, their identity must be protected; it may only be revealed if they agree to it or if it is necessary to prevent serious and imminent dangers, paragraph 6.2.1.2 of the Resolution. The aspect mentioned by Report 12006 (2009) that allegations made in bad faith trigger the protection of the whistleblower if there is sufficient public interest at stake, was not formally taken over into the Resolution. As to the Whistleblower Protection Directive, the whistleblower must equally act in good faith. The whistleblower does not have to be honest nor does the given information need to be entirely correct. However, the whistleblower must give information that he or she believes to be true at the time of the reporting.

Ultimately, though the Directive regulates a number of adjacent aspects to whistleblower protection, it does not regulate the specific relationship to the data protection right to information. The protection of personal data is mentioned in various places, such as in Art. 17 Whistleblower Protection Directive or Recitals 76 and 83 Whistleblower Protection Directive. Recital 84 Sentence 3 Whistleblower Protection Directive even provides that the Member States should ensure the effectiveness of the Whistleblower Protection Directive by restricting certain rights under the General Data Protection Regulation. The Directive does not suggest how this should be done or specify its proposal. The relationship between the data protection claim of the person concerned or accused person for

[100] Art. 23 para. 1. d) Whistleblower Protection Directive.

[101] Abazi (2020), p. 643.

information on the identity of the whistleblower and the protection of the confidentiality of the whistleblower's identity is not regulated in the Directive. Furthermore, it may be difficult for a company in practice to evaluate the requirements mentioned above and meet the obligations under the General Data Protection Regulation in a specific situation. An approach to these difficulties will be explained in further detail in **Chap. 4**.

References

Academic Articles and Contributions

Abazi V (2020) The European Union whistleblower directive: a 'Game Changer' for whistleblowing protection? Ind Law J 49(4):640

De Sousa Costa R, de Castro Ruinoinês I (2020) Preliminary remarks and practical insights on how the whistleblower protection directive adopts the GDPR principles. In: Antunes N, et al (ed) Privacy Technologies and Policy. 95

Kafteranis D (2021) The future of the whistle-blowing directive: criticising its legal bases. Queen Mary Law J 65:65

Kobron-Gasiorowska L (2022) European Union model of whistleblowing. Rev Eur Comp Law 48:191

Kostakopoulou D (2024) J'accuse!': whistleblowing, critical citizenship and the EU directive on whistleblowers' protection. J Eur Integ 46(4):477

Larmer R (2022) Whistleblowing and employee loyalty, 2. J Business Ethics 125

Leclerc O (2023) Whistleblowing legislation and reporting on research misconduct: a case for mutual learning. Account Res 32(1):1

Lewis D (2020) The EU Directive on the Protection of Whistleblowers: a Missed Opportunity to Establish International Best Practices. E-J Int Comp Labour Stud 1(9):1

Martić M (2021) Protection of the rule of law through whistleblowing. Reg Law Rev 65

Meyer F (2023) LuxLeaks, Cum-Ex & Co – new guidelines of the ECHR for whistleblowing in transnational contexts and legislative need for action. JuristenZeitung 78:261

Scheu HC (2024) Pitfalls in Implementing the EU Whistleblower Directive, Wroclaw review of law. Admin Econ 14:52

Stappers JT (2021) EU whistleblower protection directive: Europe on whistleblowing. ERA Forum 22:87

Steinhauser R, Kreis S (2021) Die Umsetzung der EU-Whistleblower-Richtlinie als Herausforderung für Gesetzgeber und Unternehmen. EuZA 422

Vandekerckhove W, Commers R (2004) Whistle blowing and rational loyalty. J Business Ethics 1–2:225

Varelius J (2008) Is whistle-blowing compatible with employee loyalty? J Business Ethics 2:263

Online Resources

Andreadakis S, Kafteranis D Halet v Luxembourg: the Final Act of the Luxleaks Saga. 21.02.2023. https://blogs.law.ox.ac.uk/oblb/blog-post/2023/02/halet-v-luxembourg-final-act-luxleaks-saga. Accessed 14 Sep 2025.

Bondarenko P In: Encyclopaedia Britannica. 29.07.2024. see: https://www.britannica.com/event/Enron-scandal. Accessed 14 Sep 2025.
Cambanza EM (2024) The Parmalat Scandal: an Analysis of Financial Deception and Its Implications for Global Business. REVES – Rev Relaç Soc 7(1):18165. https://periodicos.ufv.br/reves/article/view/18165.
George B Fraudulent Accounting and the Downfall of WorldCom, University of South Carolina, see: https://sc.edu/about/offices_and_divisions/audit_and_advisory_services/about/news/2021/worldcom_scandal.php. Accessed 14 Sep 2025.
Seventh General Activity Report of GRECO 2006, Including a Section on the "Protection of Whistleblowers", 21.03.2007, see: https://rm.coe.int/16806cb8c5. Accessed 14 Sep 2025.

Official Documents and Treaties

Cassany B (2007) Motion for a recommendation on the protection of whistleblowers, Parliamentary Assembly of the Council of Europe. Doc. 11269, 23 Apr 2007 see https://assembly.coe.int/Documents/WorkingDocs/2007/EDOC11269.pdf. Accessed 14 Sep 2025.
Civil Law Convention on Corruption, European Treaty Series No. 174, entered into force on 01 Nov 2003, further information on status and ratifications, see: https://www.coe.int/en/web/impact-convention-human-rights/civil-law-convention-on-corruption#/. Accessed 14 Sep 2025.
Committee of Ministers of the Council of Europe Recommendation CM/Rec(2014)7 on the Protection of Whistleblowers of 30 Apr 2014.
Criminal Law Convention on Corruption, European Treaty Series No. 173, entered into force on 01 July 2002, further information on status and ratifications, see: https://www.coe.int/en/web/impact-convention-human-rights/criminal-law-convention-on-corruption#/. Accessed 14 Sep 2025.
European Committee for Legal Cooperation of the Council of Europe, Feasibility Study, CDCJ (2012)9FIN of 20 Dec 2012.
European Parliament, Press Release of 16 Apr 2019, see: https://www.europarl.europa.eu/news/de/press-room/20190410IPR37529/whistleblower-neue-vorschriften-fur-eu-weiten-schutz-von-informanten. Accessed 23 Sep 2025.
Group of States against Corruption, see: https://www.coe.int/en/web/greco/home.
Omtzigt P (2009) Report 12006 on the protection of whistleblowers, Doc. 12006, 14 Sep 2009, see: https://pace.coe.int/pdf/bea4434103810f7cc0ce5478f1999185975f98219e3d4054bb302c98e93d4c17?title=Doc.%2012006.pdf. Accessed 14 Sep 2025.
Parliamentary Assembly, see: https://www.coe.int/en/web/portal/parlamentarische-versammlung#{%2214943690%22:[0]}. Accessed 14 Sep 2025.
Resolution 1729 (2010) of the Parliamentary Assembly of the Council of Europe, see: https://assembly.coe.int/nw/xml/XRef/Xref-XML2HTML-en.asp?fileid=17851. Accessed 14 Sep 2025.
Treaty Office of the Council of Europe: https://www.coe.int/fr/web/conventions/full-list?module=treaty-detail&treatynum=174.
United Nations Convention against Corruption, United Nations Treaty Series No. 2349, entered into force on 14.12.2005, see also: https://www.unodc.org/documents/brussels/UN_Convention_Against_Corruption.pdf. Accessed 14 Sep 2025.

Court Decisions

ECtHR Judg. of 11.5.2021 – 21884/18, Halet against Luxembourg
ECtHR Judg. of 12.2.2008 – 14277/04, Guja against Moldova

ECtHR Judg. of 13.1.2015 – 79040/12, Rubins against Latvia
ECtHR Judg. of 14.9.2009 – 29492/05, Kudeshkina against Russia
ECtHR Judg. of 15.2.2005 – 68416/01, Steel and Morris against the United Kingdom
ECtHR Judg. of 16.2.2021 – 23922/19, Gawlik against Liechtenstein
ECtHR Judg. of 17.9.2015 – 14464/11, Langner against Germany
ECtHR Judg. of 19.1.2016 – 12138/08, Aurelian Opera against Romania
ECtHR Judg. of 21.6.2016 – 79972/12, Soares against Portugal
ECtHR Judg. of 21.7.2011 – 28274/08, Heinisch against Germany
ECtHR Judg. of 25.4.1978 – 5856/72, Tyrer against the United Kingdom
ECtHR Judg. of 26.4.1979 – 6538/74, Sunday Times (No. 1) against the United Kingdom
ECtHR Judg. of 27.11.2007 – 20477/05, Tillack against Belgium
ECtHR Judg. of 29.2.2000 – 39293/98, Fuentes Bobo against Spain
ECtHR Judg. of 5.9.2017 – 61496/08, Barbulescu against Romania
ECtHR Judg. of 7.12.1976 – 5493/72, Handyside against the United Kingdom
ECtHR Judg. of 8.1.2013 – 40238/02, Bucur and Roma against Romania
ECtHR Judg. of 8.12.2010 – 28955/06, 28957/06, 28959/06, 28964/06, Palomo Sánchez and others against Spain
ECtHR Judg. of 12.10.2010 – 49001/07, Bathellier against France
ECtHR Judg. of 15.11.2012 – 53579/09 and 53582/09, Bargao and Domingos Correia against Portugal
ECtHR Judg. of 18.10.2011 – 10247/09, Sosinowska against Poland
ECtHR Judg. of 21.10.2014 – 73571/10, Matuz against Hungary

Chapter 3
The Right of Access under European Data Protection Law

In the current regime of European data protection law, the General Data Protection Regulation (GDPR) is the dominating legal foundation. The right to data protection is enshrined in Art. 8 EU Charter and constitutes a fundamental right. This fundamental right is regarded as a right that is separate from the right to privacy, which is provided for in Art. 7 EU Charter. As the right to data protection has become such a cornerstone in the area of digital rights and daily life, the GDPR sets up more concrete and more concrete and strict rules. A very important part of the protective rules of the GDPR are the data subject rights. Of these rights, arguably the most essential claim for data subjects is the right of access to their data. The rationale behind the right of access is to give data subjects the chance to gain insight to the data controller's cache of data about them. Through this right, data subjects have a claim against the data controller to compel them show or hand over all personal data regarding the data subject. This right aims at reducing the secrecy or the so-called "black box character" of data processing. At the same time, it provides the basis for other rights of the data subject under the GDPR, such as the right to rectification, the right to restriction of data processing and the right to erasure. Legally, the right to access arises from Art. 15 GDPR, making it the central data protection instrument at the EU level. Even in the context of European human rights law a general right to access is enshrined in Art. 9 para. 1 lit. b Convention 108 + . Convention 108 + is an international treaty construed under the auspices of the Council of Europe and following the Convention 108 from 1985. The renewed convention is open for ratification since 2018. In the following, the focus will be on the GDPR as it has turned out the more effective legal framework in this area.

In greater detail, the right to access under Art. 15 GDPR requires a data controller to comply with a catalogue of specific requirements once a data subject has requested access. The controller has to inform the data subject i.a. about the

S. Koloßa, *Whistleblower Protection and the Right of Access*, SpringerBriefs in Law,
https://doi.org/10.1007/978-3-032-04817-2_3

purposes of the data processing,[1] the categories of processed data,[2] and also the source of the collected personal data.[3] This legal provision has been at the core of various legal discussions that have already led to prominent decisions by the European Court of Justice (ECJ).[4] Thus, the essential focus in the context of the whistleblower protection shall lie on Art. 15 para. 1. g) GDPR which stipulates the right to gain information about the source of processed data. If the respective personal data is not gathered from the data subject, he or she is has a right to know from whence the data was collected. This aspect of the right to access is particularly challenging for the confidentiality of a whistleblower's identity as the controller is basically under an obligation to reveal it per Art. 15 para. 1. g) GDPR. The following sections will shed light on the questions of applicability of the right of access under the GDPR in this context as well as its requirements vis-à-vis the identity of the whistleblower—as this right directly conflicts with the whistleblower's right to confidentiality.

3.1 Applicability of the Data Protection Access Claim in the Employment Relationship

The right of access under the GDPR generally applies between the affected person, the so-called data subject according to Art. 4 No. 1 GDPR, and the controller. According to Art. 4 No. 7 GDPR, the controller is any natural or legal person, authority, institution or other body that alone or together with others decides on the purposes and means of processing of personal data. A company, therefore, in the role of an employer, is responsible for ensuring compliance with data protection obligations as it relates to the processing of the personal data of its employees. In the context of employment matters, the GDPR provides for an enabling clause in Art. 88 GDPR but this does not mean that the main and essential rights of a data subject, such as the right of access, are to be limited. The right to access regularly applies to an employment relationship.[5]

According to Art. 2 para. 1 GDPR, the regulation applies to the whole or partially automated processing of personal data as well as to the non-automated processing of personal data that are to be stored in a filing system. According to

[1] Art. 15 para. 1. a) GDPR.

[2] Art. 15 para. 1. b) GDPR.

[3] Art. 15 para. 1. g) GDPR.

[4] See e.g. ECJ Ruling of 27.5.2024—C-312/23, Addiko Bank; ECJ Judg. of 4.5.2023—C-487/21, ECLI:EU:C:2023:369.

[5] Cf. e.g. ECJ, Judg. of 30.3.2023—C-34/21, ECLI:EU:C:2023:270; this has also been confirmed by national court decisions, e.g. in Germany: Federal Labour Court (BAG), Judg. of 16.12.2021–2 AZR 235/21, also in: NZA 2022, p. 362; Regional Labour Court (LAG) Baden-Württemberg, Judg. of 20.12.2018–17 Sa 11/18, para. 220.

Art. 4 No. 6 GDPR, a filing system refers to any structured collection of personal data that is accessible according to certain criteria, regardless of whether this collection is central, decentralised or organised according to functional or geographical aspects. The employer processes countless employee data in the course of the execution of the employment relationship and the reporting system under the whistleblower protection regime constitutes a structured collection of data. Thus, here the employer processes even more data.

Accordingly, there is no doubt that the right of access to personal data applies in the context of an allegation by a whistleblower report that is collected and investigated by the employer.

3.2 Relationship Between the GDPR and the Whistleblower Protection Directive

At first glance, the relation between the GDPR and the Whistleblower Protection Directive appears simple. Both are legal acts under the EU legal framework, one having the form of a directive, the other the form of a regulation in the meaning of Art. 288 Treaty of the Functioning of the EU. However, the Whistleblower Protection Directive does not have to conform with the GDPR as the GDPR is not a higher law above the Directive.[6] Moreover, it is argued that the Whistleblower Protection Directive is a legitimate exception in the meaning of Art. 23 para. 1. i) GDPR.[7] This provision allows for a deviation or restriction of i.a. the right of access under Art. 15 GDPR provided this deviation is based on another law that respects the essence of the fundamental rights and freedoms and is a necessary and proportionate measure in a democratic society to carefully safeguard the protection of the data subject and the rights and freedoms of others. The Whistleblower Protection Directive, however, also explicitly mentions that "[a]ny processing of personal data carried out pursuant to this Directive, including the exchange or transmission of personal data by the competent authorities, should be undertaken in accordance with Regulation (EU) 2016/679".[8] Furthermore, it stipulates that "[t]he effective protection of the confidentiality of the identity of reporting persons is necessary for the protection of the rights and freedoms of others, in particular those of the reporting persons, provided for under point (i) of Article 23(1) of Regulation (EU) 2016/679".[9] Nevertheless, not all behaviour of

---

[6] Kämmerer, Redder (2025) German Whistleblower Protection Act, Sec. 1 para. 43 et seq.

[7] See also German Parliament Document 20/3442, p. 74; Reufels, Soltysiak (2023), p. 98; extensively Bruns (2025), Sec. 8 para. 25 et seq. with further sources especially in the context of Art. 19 Whistleblower Protection Directive.

[8] Recital 83 Sentence 1 Whistleblower Protection Directive.

[9] Recital 84 Sentence 2 Whistleblower Protection Directive.

a whistleblower grants the person the relevant protection.[10] This shows that both legal interests, the right of access and the confidentiality of the whistleblower must be balanced carefully as both are of the highest value.[11]

3.3 Hints in the Sense of Whistleblower Protection as Personal Data

In the context of a whistleblower's report, the given hints about potential violations are usually connected to a specific person committing the violations. It may be the case that the person is specifically and directly named as part of an allegation by the whistleblower. If so, there is a direct link between that information and the data subject, and the information constitutes personal data in the sense of Art. 4 No. 1 GDPR. Additionally, even if the whistleblower does not mention the potential perpetrator explicitly by name but rather there is a set of information, such as descriptions of situations or other specific context, which nevertheless leads to the data subject in the sense that the data subject can be identified, then the information equally constitutes personal data. According to the European Court of Justice, the term "personal data" is to be understood broadly.[12] It is by no means limited to sensitive or private information. Rather, the broad concept of personal data essentially encompasses all types of information of both an objective and subjective nature, which can be presented in the form of opinions as well as assessments. For example, although descriptions of circumstances, such as general grievances, often do not constitute personal data in an abstract sense, the reference to a person is established when these grievances are presented in the context of a specific person, thus they are information about the person in question. The latter condition is always met when the information is linked to a specific person due to its content, purpose or effects.[13] After all, the mere description of a (potential) misconduct in general is not necessarily connected to a specific individual and may not immediately constitute personal data. However, the data becomes personal data, for instance, when the described misconduct is focusing on a specific person, who subsequently becomes the subject of the internal investigation. Generally, if the whistleblower's report cannot be evaluated properly by the internal reporting office of an enterprise because its allegations are too vague or too broad, this leads to further procedures, namely follow-up measures. According to Article 9 para. 1. d) Whistleblower Protection Directive, internal

[10] See Chapter 1 above.

[11] Mengel (2023), Sec. 7, para. 58; Dzida, Granetzny (2020), p. 1205 et seq; International Bar Association (2018), p. 25 et seq.

[12] ECJ, Judg. of 7.3.2024—C-604/22, ECLI:EU:C:2024:214, para. 35 et seq.; ECJ, Judg. of 20.12.2017—C-434/16, ECLI:EU:C:2017:994, para. 33–35; ECJ, Judg. of 19.10.2016—C-582/14, ECLI:EU:C:2017:563, para. 32 et seq.

[13] See e.g. EDPB (2019), p. 7; Art. 29 Working Party Opinion (2007), p. 6 et seq.; German Federal Court (BGH), Judgement of 22.2.2022—VI ZR 14/21, para. 11.

reporting requires a diligent follow-up by the designated department. A follow-up in the sense of Article 5 para. 12 Whistleblower Protection Directive means, inter alia, any action taken by the recipient of a report to assess the accuracy of the allegations made in the report. The aim of such follow-up is not only to build trust in the effectiveness of the overall system of whistleblower protection,[14] but also to prepare the adequate next steps that may lead to a referral to other channels, a closure of the proceedings or the start of an internal investigation.[15] In the end, however, the required follow-up will basically always include the focus on a specific person, the data subject, as the proceedings of whistleblower protection foresee it.

3.4 Information on the Identity of the Whistleblower

Art. 15 para. 1 GDPR stipulates that a data subject may request confirmation from the controller as to whether the controller is processing data about them. If this is the case, the data subject may request further information on the processed data.

In this context, the mandatory information the controller must provide is listed in the catalogue of Art. 15 para. 1 sentence 2 GDPR. This catalogue provides under g) the obligation of the controller to disclose to the data subject any information about the source or origin of the processed data in the event that the controller has not gathered the data from the data subject themselves.

3.4.1 Data Collection by the Controller

In the context of whistleblower reporting, the question arises whether the report by the whistleblower constitutes data collection by the controller. It could be argued that it was not the controller who collected the data, but rather it was the whistleblower, who imposed the data on the controller. If this argument were convincing, the claim from Art. 15. para 1. g) GDPR could be dismissed. Art. 15. Para 1. g) GDPR explicitly restricts the obligation to inform on the origin of data to such data that the controller collected from other sources than the data subjects themselves.[16] However, both the notion of processing data as well as the collection of data, are to be interpreted broadly.[17] Already in its Google Spain decision, the ECJ stated that: "In exploring the internet automatically, constantly and systematically in search of the information which is published there, the operator of a search engine 'collects' such data which it subsequently 'retrieves',

[14] Rec. 57 Sentence 1 Whistleblower Protection Directive.

[15] Rec. 57 Sentence 3 Whistleblower Protection Directive.

[16] Considered, but finally denied in German Federal Court (BGH), Judg. of 22.2.2022—VI ZR 14/21, para. 18.

[17] See e.g. Papakonstantinou, De Hert (2023), para. 36.

'records' and 'organizes' within the framework of its indexing programmes, 'stores' on its servers and, as the case may be, 'discloses' and 'makes available' to its users in the form of lists of search results, which constitute processing, regardless of the fact that the operator of the search engine also carries out the same operations in respect of other types of information and does not distinguish between the latter and the personal data".[18] The controller collects data whenever it stores such data for organizing, preparing for further processing and other purposes, and even if the fate of such data is not yet determined at the moment of the collection. In the context of the whistleblower protection, an enterprise has to deal with allegations and information it receives, even if the information is later discarded due to a lack of substance or some other reasons. An allegation made by the notifying person, the whistleblower, is to be considered data collection by the controller in the sense of Art. 15. para 1. g) GDPR.

Not directly decided in the context of whistleblowing or the right to access, yet still relevant here, is the ruling by the ECJ confirming that the processing of personal data may also include oral communication as long as the data is already part of or intended to be part of a filing system in the meaning of Art. 2 para. 1 GDPR.[19] The ECJ broadened the applicability of the GDPR in general and the notion of processing—which includes the data collection—to certain information given viva voce. Regarding the protection of the whistleblower's identity, the question of whether to disclose the origin of allegations and all the information related to it, would mean including such information that is not yet entered into a whistleblower reporting system—but still has the status of an oral complaint—as long as it is intended to be formally reported in a type of filing system. These situations are included in the whistleblower protection and form part of the broad interpretation of the data collected by the controller.

3.4.2 *Addressee of the Right of Access*

Under Art. 15 para 1. g), the addressee of the right of access is the controller of the data in question. The controller is the entity which determines the purpose and means of the processing of personal data.[20] Normally, the data subject would address his or her employer and claim the data. Yet, whether the employer is indeed the right addressee in the context of typical whistleblower protection situations, requires a closer look.

3.4.2.1 Preparation of a Whistleblower Report

The reporting process of a potential misconduct may be separated into two phases, the preparation phase of the report and the actual reporting. In the preparation

---

[18] ECJ Judg. of 13.5.2014—C-131/12, ECLI:EU:C:2013:424, para. 28.

[19] ECJ Judg. of 7.3.2024—C-740/22, ECLI:EU:C:2024:216, para. 25 et seq.

[20] See definition in Art. 4 No. 7 GDPR.

phase, the whistleblower may—depending on the specific situation—conduct his or her own investigations and collect information including personal data.[21] Especially if these pre-investigations entail the use of text editors to electronically collect the information or taking pictures or videos of the respective actions, the whistleblower is collecting data in a type of filing system within the meaning of Art. 2 para. 1 GDPR and the material scope of the GDPR is triggered.[22] Initially, when the whistleblower collects data for his or her own purposes, including to be able to file a proper and concise report, the whistleblower acts as data controller for such data.[23] At first, it is only the whistleblower who pursues the aim of preparing a report. Hence, it is the whistleblower who determines the purposes and means of the processing of personal data relating to the report and acts within the capacity as a data controller in the meaning of Art. 4 para. 7 GDPR. This also means that the whistleblower is obliged to bear the responsibilities of the controllership position, at least until the he or she uses the reporting tool and files the report. Until that moment, the actual employer does not act as an (additional) controller. So the crucial question is when does the employer become the right addressee for the general claim of the right of access.

3.4.2.2 Internal Reporting

Typically, the controllership usually shifts away from the whistleblower as soon as the whistleblower files the report through the internal reporting channels—the employer's technical infrastructure established for the purpose of creating a whistleblower reporting system. At first, it is still the whistleblower who enters the data in the reporting system and the whistleblower decides which data he or she provides. Nevertheless, the technical channels, which information is requested, how it is processed, the information management, and ultimately the decision upon the purposes and means remains with the employer. The employer typically chooses between general and specialized channels. The general channels may entail email, phone or direct personal contact with the reporting department[24] while specialized channels can be web-based platforms, call centres, or mobile apps.[25]

The controllership status is a functional concept.[26] When determining the controllership, it is important to consider the unique circumstances of each case rather than adhere to a strict, formal analysis.[27] The evaluation of the information

---

[21] Cf. in general for the whistleblower's perspective: Bishop-Monroe, Harrison (2021), p. 3.

[22] Musiol (2024), p. 8.

[23] Musiol (2024), p. 8.

[24] Whistleblower Report 2021, p. 44 et seq.; Dendorfer-Ditges (2025), Sec. 75, para. 160; Whistleblowing Report 2021, p. 44 et seq.

[25] Whistleblower Report 2021, p. 44 et seq.; Dendorfer-Ditges (2025), Sec. 75, para. 160.

[26] EDPB, Guidelines 07/2020, para. 21.

[27] EDPB, Guidelines 07/2020, para. 21.

received, and especially the internal investigations which the employer must commence as a reaction to the allegations made, are so-called follow-up measures in the meaning of Art. 5 para. 12 Whistleblower Protection Directive.[28] Art. 5 para. 12 Whistleblower Protection Directive defines follow-ups as "any action taken by the recipient of a report or any competent authority, to assess the accuracy of the allegations made in the report and, where relevant, to address the breach reported, including through actions such as an internal enquiry, an investigation, prosecution, an action for recovery of funds, or the closure of the procedure".[29] The entity that determines and conducts the follow-up measures is the employer, not the whistleblower employee. Therefore, the whistleblower is not an active party for the processing of personal data in the sense that would allow the whistleblower to act as another controller.

The whistleblower is neither a separate controller, nor is he or she a joint controller together with the employer. The joint controllership is a specific constellation under the GDPR where two or more controllers jointly determine the purposes and means of processing.[30] The joint participation in the determination of the means and purposes requires that all respective entities have a decisive influence over the if and the how of the processing.[31] The cooperation in this sense may stem from a common decision or a converging decision.[32] Whereas a common decision is rather simple to establish, the criterion of converging decisions is more complex. According to the European Data Protection Board (EDPB), one criteria to determine converging decisions as to the means and purposes of the processing is if the decisions "complement each other and are necessary for the processing to take place in such manner that they have a tangible impact on the determination of the purposes and means of the processing".[33] In other words, it should be analysed whether the processing would not be possible without both parties' joint participation so that the processing of both parties is inextricably linked and, as such, inseparable.[34] However, it is not necessary for both parties to have equal access to the data in question. The ECJ decided e.g. that a religious group establishes joint controllership together with its preaching members about the personal data that the members collect in their door-to-door preaching.[35] Granted, this definition seems hard to deploy as one could argue that the employer could not instigate any investigations without the hint by the whistleblower. Yet, at the same time, it seems odd to regard both the whistleblower and the employer as joint controllers.

[28] Cf. for general introduction to internal investigations under the Whistleblower Protection Directive i.a. Dilling (2020), p. 136 ff.

[29] For control stemming from legal provisions, see: EDPB, Guidelines 07/2020, para. 22 et seq.

[30] Art. 26 para. 1 sentence 1 GDPR.

[31] EDPB, Guidelines 07/2020, para. 54.

[32] EDPB, Guidelines 07/2020, para. 55.

[33] EDPB, Guidelines 07/2020, para. 55.

[34] EDPB, Guidelines 07/2020, para. 55.

[35] ECJ Judg. of 10.7.2018—C-25/17, ECLI:EU:C:2018:551, para. 75.

In fact, the role of the whistleblower is exclusively to provide information. After a whistleblower provides that information, the measures that follow are conducted by an impartial internal investigator or department that stays in contact with the whistleblower and may ask for further clarification.[36] The actual investigation is not determined by the whistleblower so that the whistleblower is not a controller jointly with the employer.

Another question concerns the controllership of the actual employer. As previously noted, an independent person or department within the company shall conduct the investigations under the Whistleblower Protection Directive. This could lead to the conclusion that such internal entity assumes the role of a controller, independent of their employer relationship with the actual employer. A comparable situation exists for the works council within a company. The council assumes independent functions that include those not entirely in the interest of the company and its management board. The investigation is supposed to be conducted independently which includes the work against the prima facie interest of the management board and maybe the company. In the case of Germany, the question of the controllership of the workers council has been answered by the German legislature. Sec. 79a Sentence 2 German Works Constitution Act stipulates that the employer remains the data controller in the meaning of the GDPR, if the works council acts within its given competences. This legislative solution is not without its caveats.[37] On the one hand, this solution appears aligned with the general rule under the GDPR that any person acting under the authority of the controller will not assume their own controllership position.[38] Employees of a controller—be they also part of the works council, be they part of the investigative team for investigating allegations by a whistleblower—remain employees and thus it is suitable to argue that only the employer acts as the controller. On the other hand, the controllership position under the GDPR is established as a role. This role is not a fixed position such as the position of an employee. An employee acting ultra vires is regarded as an act outside of the authority of the employer's directives under Art. 29 GDPR and, as a result, that employee takes over the controllership position for the transgression of his or her actual functions and duties. An internal investigative team could just as well be deemed controller of the data processing. The bigger picture sees the employer more in the exclusive controller position. In contrast to the work council, the internal whistleblower reporting entity may ask questions or try to collect information about the factual background of the allegation. Yet, the internal entity normally has no competence to enact legal consequences. The competence to take measures against a misconduct lies with the employer.[39] However, the general liability of the employer for breach of obligations under

[36] Cf. Art. 9 para. 1 lit. c Whistleblower Protection Directive.

[37] For a critical view on Sec. 79a German Works Constitution Act see e.g. Maschmann (2021).

[38] Cf. Art. 29 GDPR.

[39] Dendorfer-Ditges (2025), Sec. 75, para. 166.

the GDPR by its employees has also been confirmed by the ECJ.[40] In this context, and for the question of the whistleblower protection against the right of access, the employer shall be deemed the exclusive controller.

Lastly, the employer also could engage an external entity with such a task, whereas this entity is not considered an external reporting authority within the meaning of Art. 10 et seq. Whistleblower Protection Directive. Such a third party could be external reporting platform providers, external counsel, auditors, trade union representatives or employees' representatives.[41] This third party could assume the role of the internal channel. If this is the case, the outsourced internal entity usually acts as the data processor according to Art. 28 GDPR and is under the final supervision of the employer. Also in this situation, the employer remains the controller, and a request of data access is to be addressed to the employer.

3.4.2.3 External Reporting

The Whistleblower Protection Directive foresees external reporting mechanisms as a second channel for addressing whistleblower information. External reporting entities are authorities of the Member States according to Art. 11 para. 2 Whistleblower Protection Directive. The competent authorities are not acting under the supervision of the employer; they are entirely remote and outside of the organization of the employer.[42] They conduct their investigations under their own auspices, stipulated by the relevant national law. In such cases, they decide the means and purposes of the data processing and take the role as exclusive controllers. Hence, they are the correct addressees for the right of access under Art. 15 GDPR.

3.4.2.4 Public Proclamation

The Whistleblower Protection Directive also foresees the option for a whistleblower to address the public through online platforms or social media, or through the media, elected officials, civil society organizations, trade unions, or professional and business organizations.[43] Public disclosures in the meaning of Art. 15 Whistleblower Protection Directive are an allowed and protected means of a whistleblowing channel only if i.a. the internal or external reporting has had no effect and no appropriate action has been taken, and, moreover, the whistleblower has reason to believe that there is an imminent or manifest danger to the public interest, such as where there is an emergency situation or a risk of irreversible damage. In such situations, neither an internal nor an external channel is

[40] ECJ Judg. of 11.4.2024—C-741/21, ECLI:EU:C:2024:288.

[41] See Recital 54 Sentence 2 Whistleblower Protection Directive.

[42] Cf. Recital 45 Whistleblower Protection Directive.

[43] Cf. Recital 45 Whistleblower Protection Directive.

meaningfully involved in the data processing that comes with the public disclosure. Thus, the whistleblower will remain the responsible data controller, potentially jointly with another third party involved such as a whistleblower platform.[44] In this instance, right of access under Art. 15 GDPR is useless as the origin of the publicly disclosed personal data is directly apparent.

3.4.2.5 Interim Result: Controllership Situations

In brief, the question of the controllership in the whistleblower context is not a trivial one. At first, the whistleblower controls a data collection under his or her own agenda when preparing a report and gathering information including their own possible research endeavours. As soon as the whistleblower reports the data to an external authority, the controllership shifts to that authority. In the case of internal reporting, the question is most complex and the entity, in the form of an internal investigator or a department, or the employer in general, could gain the controllership. For the sake of answering the primary question of this undertaking, the employer is assumed to act as data controller in the case of an internal reporting. In contrast, in the case of a public disclosure, the whistleblower remains the formal controller, potentially jointly with a third party such as a whistleblower platform.

3.4.3 Brief Overview of the Historical Development of the Right of Access and Its Content

The exact wording of the EU legal draft provisions on the right of access were changed and adapted several times during legislative procedures.[45] The various draft texts differed considerably in some cases.

The right of access as such was included already in the mid-1990s in the "Directive 95/46/EC of the European Parliament and of the Council of 24 October 1995 on the protection of individuals with regard to the processing of personal data and on the free movement" (Data Protection Directive), the predecessor to the GDPR. Specifically, Art. 12. a) 2nd dash Data Protection Directive gave the data subject the right to receive a notification of "available information about the origin of the data". This claim to the origin information was by no means self-evident. In the original proposal of the Commission

[44] See on the matter of joint controllership with several parties involved also ECJ Judg. of 11.1.2024—C-231/22, ECLI:EU:C:2024:7.

[45] Schmidt-Wudy (2023), Art. 15 GDPR, para. 1; Paal (2021) Art. 15 GDPR, para. 2; Bräutigam, Schmidt-Wudy (2015), p. 1.

(GDPR-COM) there was only a general right of access to the processed personal data.[46] The subsequent proposal of the Parliament (GDPR-EP) brought clarifications of the right to information among other things in such a way that there was also a claim to the origin information.[47] In the Council (GDPR-Council) several delegations intended to limit the rights to information to a minimum.[48] It was even argued that the right to information about the origin of the data should be eliminated completely, even if such origin information was available.[49] Ultimately, the conviction prevailed that the origin of the data can be of essential importance for the person concerned and thus they received a claim in Art. 12. a) 2nd dash Data Protection Directive.

The original proposal of the EU Commission for the GDPR of 25 January 2012 went beyond the wording of the Data Protection Directive. In Art. 15 para. 1 sentence 2. g) GDPR-COM it was stated that the controller must inform the data subject on all data "as well as all available information about the origin of the data". Interestingly, this obligation of the controller was excluded in the legislative resolution of the European Parliament on the Commission's proposal of 12 March 2014. A justification for the exclusion cannot be found, neither in the draft report of 16 January 2013 nor in the report of the European Parliament of 22 November 2013. Similarly, there was no explanation formally recorded for the deletion of this part.[50]

One could speculate that, from the perspective of the European Parliament, the right to know the origin of one's data is already included in Art. 14 para. 3 GDPR-EP. This provision said "If the personal data are not collected from the data subject, the controller for processing informs this person, in addition to the information mentioned in paragraph 1, of the origin of the specific personal data". Some voices in the literature also view this interpretation critically.[51] A final explanation of the reasons is therefore no longer possible. However, the argument put forward is significantly countered by the fact that a comparable obligation to inform about the origin was already anchored in Art. 14 para. 3 GDPR-COM.

In the draft of the Council of the European Union (hereinafter: Council) the deletion was then reversed. The Council made a restriction, namely, to limit the indication of the origin of the data to the case that the data collection was not carried out by the data subject himself. This version was finally approved in the trilogue procedure and adopted in the final version of Art. 15 GDPR as it reads today.

[46] Grabitz, Hilf (2009), Art. 12, para. 2.

[47] Grabitz, Hilf (2009), Art. 12, para. 3.

[48] Grabitz, Hilf (2009), Art. 12, para. 4.

[49] Grabitz, Hilf (2009), Art. 12, para. 4.

[50] See only Liedke (2014), p. 714.

[51] Bräutigam, Schmidt-Wudy (2015), p. 1; Liedke (2014), p. 714.

3.4.4 *Scope of the Claim to Get to Know the Origin of the Processed Data*

The right of access under Art. 15 GDPR is considered the heart of the data protection rights of the data subject. Partly, the right of access under Art. 15 GDPR together with the information obligations of the controller under Art. 13 and 14 GDPR is regarded as the "Magna Carta" of the rights of the data subject.[52] The right of access is of such outstanding importance because it substantiates the basic right of access to data under Art. 8 para. 2 of the Charter of Fundamental Rights of the European Union. Moreover, only such information provided by the controller puts a data subject in a capable position to gain knowledge of all the data processing conducted by the controller. Once in that position, the data subject is able to assess whether the data processing is lawful and possibly assert further rights such as the right to rectification (Art. 16 GDPR), right to erasure (Art. 17 GDPR) or the right to data portability (Art. 20 GDPR).[53] Therefore, the purpose of the right of access exists primarily to create transparency in the processing procedures of personal data.[54] This is additionally anchored in Recital 63 of the GDPR. Nevertheless, the provision of Art. 15 para. 1. g) GDPR requires interpretation.

According to the wording of the provision, the data subject has a right to all available information about the origin of the data processed by the data controller, provided that the personal data were not collected from the data subject himself. The ambiguity of the wording refers specifically to the characteristic of data collection by the controller. It may be disputed whether the company must deliberately record the hint received from the whistleblower for it to be considered a collection in the meaning of Art. 15 para. 1. g) GDPR, or whether it is sufficient if the company merely accepts it.

In order to illustrate the legal issues and reasoning in this context, a German case may be helpful. In a case decided by the German Federal Court of Justice a rental dispute was at issue, in which one party in a multi-family house complained to their landlord about another tenant.[55] The complaint concerned an alleged strong odour nuisance and vermin in the stairwell. After the landlord approached the affected tenant and demanded the removal of the nuisance, the tenant reacted indignantly and sought information about the identity of the person from whom the complaint originated. As the basis for his claim, he invoked Art. 15 para. 1. g) GDPR.

The court of first instance, the Ravensburg Regional Court, argued that the landlord had not collected the aspects of the odour nuisance and the vermin in the stairwell himself, but had been alerted to this by a co-tenant. Data collection

[52] Dix (2023), Art. 15 GDPR, para. 1; Schmidt-Wudy (2023), Art. 15 GDPR, para. 2.

[53] See e.g. ECJ Judgement of 12.1.2023—C-154/21 ECLI:EU:C:2023:3, para. 30 et seq.

[54] Schmidt-Wudy (2023), Art. 15 GDPR, para. 2.

[55] German Federal Court (BGH), Judg. of 22.2.2022—VI ZR 14/21, p. 326.

requires an active action. The landlord had not obtained this information through active action, but only had passively accepted it, as it was communicated to him by another tenant. From this, the Ravensburg Regional Court concluded that the landlord had not collected this data in the sense of Art. 15 para. 1. g) GDPR. It judged the facts of the right to information as unfulfilled so it did not grant the plaintiff a right to be informed about the origin of the data and it did not oblige the landlord to name the author of the complaint.[56]

The claim from Art. 15 para. 1. g) GDPR is read within the context of Art. 13 and 14 GDPR. Where Art. 15 GDPR enshrines the right to information, Art. 13 and 14 GDPR embody information rights in favour of the data subject. The information rights generally refer to the time of data collection, with Art. 14 GDPR setting out the information obligations in the event that the data are not collected from the data subject himself.

In the second instance of the aforementioned case, the German Stuttgart Higher Regional Court stated that the systematics of Art. 13, 14 and 15 GDPR suggest to affirm a collection.[57] Art. 14 GDPR, in contrast to Art. 13 GDPR and simultaneously parallel to Art. 15 para. 1. g) GDPR, refers to collection from third parties. This would suggest a broad interpretation of the characteristic "collection" in the sense of data receipt.

This also is indicated by sentence 1 of Recital 63 to the GDPR, which states: "A data subject should have a right of access to personal data that have been collected, and should be able to exercise this right easily and at reasonable intervals, in order to be aware of and verify the lawfulness of the processing." The Stuttgart Higher Regional Court concluded that Art. 15 para. 1. g) GDPR is intended to cover the cases of Art. 14 GDPR, which claim a general right of access to the data subject except if he or she is the source of the data.[58]

This view is not entirely convincing because the information obligations from Art. 13 and 14 GDPR usually provide information *ex ante*, so the wording may have a different content within the scope of Art. 15 GDPR, which refers to the data processing *ex post*.

The German Federal Court was of the opinion that it does not make sense for the controller to withhold the origin of information from the data subject in the context of whistleblower cases, when information about a person is brought to the attention of the controller, and he then actually uses it.

Many voices in academia share this view.[59] Schmidt-Wudy argues that Art. 15 para. 1. g) GDPR always requires "all available information about the origin" of the data.[60] The only prerequisite for the claim is that the controller holds data of the data subject and that this data was not collected from the data subject directly.

[56] Higher Regional Court (OLG) Stuttgart, Judg. of 10.12.2020–13 U 278/20, para. 45 et seq.

[57] Higher Regional Court (OLG) Stuttgart, Judg. of 10.12.2020–13 U 278/20, para. 47.

[58] Higher Regional Court (OLG) Stuttgart, Judg. of 10.12.2020–13 U 278/20, para. 47.

[59] See e.g. Schmidt-Wudy (2023), Art. 15 GDPR, para. 74; Franck (2022) Art. 15, para. 16; Paal (2021), Art. 15, para. 30.

[60] Schmidt-Wudy (2023), Art. 15 GDPR, para. 74.

In the case mentioned above, the German Federal Court finally confirmed this. According to Art. 15 para. 1. g) GDPR, all available information is owed, including, in principle, the identity of the whistleblower.[61] The fact that the data was brought to the attention of the controller by the whistleblower without the controller's request, and the controller did not actively obtain the data from him, is irrelevant for the right to information about the origin of the data.[62] What is decisive is that the controller processes the data in a targeted manner. He does this simply because he follows-up on the hint.

The heavy weight of the right to information also lies in the fact that it does not stand alone but is anchored in fundamental rights. In Art. 8 EU Charter of Fundamental Rights, the fundamental right to data protection is expressly established alongside the right to respect for private life in Art. 7 EU Charter of Fundamental Rights. The right to information is of such central importance that it is even expressly mentioned in Art. 8 para. 2 sentence 2 GDPR.

It is to be agreed with that the identity of the whistleblower also falls under the origin of the data according to Art. 15 para. 1. g) GDPR. Even if the wording and the systematics do not allow a clear classification, the purpose of the right to access can only be fulfilled if the claim exists. The data subject can only make an informed decision about whether to exercise further data subject rights if he or she can learn the identity of the whistleblower.

3.5 Limits of the Right of Access

The right of access is not granted without restrictions. For example, Art. 15 para. 4 GDPR already contains an explicit inherent limit—the rights and freedoms of others when receiving a copy of the data. Sometimes, other legal regimes explicitly mention restrictions to the right of access such as Art. 41 para. 4 Anti Money Laundering Directive (Directive (EU) 2015/849). Another limit can result from an abusive assertion of the claim. A third limit arises in the case where the disclosure of the identity of the whistleblower to the affected person itself constitutes data processing requiring justification in the context of Art. 4 No. 2 GDPR. In these cases, a reason in the sense of Art. 6 para. 1 GDPR must be present.

[61] German Federal Court (BGH), Judg. of 22.2.2022—VI ZR 14/21 para. 8.

[62] German Federal Court (BGH), Judg. of 22.2.2022—VI ZR 14/21 para. 13.

3.5.1 *Limit Due to an Adverse Effect of the Rights and Freedoms of Others, Art. 15 para. 4 GDPR*

The only limit expressly mentioned in Art. 15 GDPR of the right to information can be found in Art. 15 para. 4 GDPR. It explicitly states that the right to receive a copy of the data in the sense of Art. 15 para. 3 GDPR must not infringe the rights and freedoms of others. By its wording, this restriction only applies to the claim for copies of the data, not to the general right to information under Art. 15 para. 1. g) GDPR. Nevertheless, it is the prevailing view that the restriction of paragraph 4 may apply to the several aspects of the right of access. In part, the wording of Art. 15 para. 4 GDPR is assumed to be an editorial error.[63] The remaining views rightly see the conditions for a legal analogy as fulfilled.[64] This is confirmed by Recital 63 para. 5 GDPR, which states that the right to information should not infringe the rights and freedoms of other persons, such as trade secrets or intellectual property rights and, in particular, the copyright on software. Unfortunately, the European Data Protection Board (EDPB) has issued a misleading guideline on this issue. According to the EDPB, the exception of Art. 15 para. 4 GDPR is not applicable to the additional information under Art. 15 para. 1. a)—h) GDPR, hence it cannot be used to protect the identity of the whistleblower.[65] However, the EDPB also stated that applying the exception of Art. 15 para. 4 GDPR shall not result in denying the request under Art. 15 GDPR, "it would only result in leaving out or rendering illegible those parts that may have negative effects for the rights and freedoms of others".[66] The more plausible interpretation would confirm that relying on the reasons of Art. 15 para. 4 GDPR must not lead to a generalized denial of the claims under Art. 15 para. 1 GDPR. As the EDPB also stated, the controller must demonstrate that the rights and freedoms of others would be adversely affected in each specific situation.[67] Also the Whistleblower Protection Directive has foreseen the clash of the rights of access and whistleblower protection but has explicitly stated in Recital 84 Whistleblower Protection Directive: "The effective protection of the confidentiality of the identity of reporting persons is necessary for the protection of the rights and freedoms of others, in particular those of the reporting persons provided for under [. . .] Regulation (EU) 2016/679", namely the GDPR. Nevertheless, no explicit exception is mentioned specifically with regard to the protection of the whistleblower in the operational part of the Directive.

Furthermore, in a case outside the context of whistleblower protection, the ECJ already found that the identity of other persons than the data subject and the controller generally is to be protected. In that case, the ECJ found that a data

[63] Bienemann (2022), Art. 15, para. 57.

[64] Schmidt-Wudy (2023), Art. 15, para. 96 et seq.; Dix (2023), Art. 15, para. 34 et seq.; Franck (2022), Art. 15, para. 33 et seq.; Paal (2021), Art. 15, para. 41; Stollhoff (2020), Art. 15, para. 38.

[65] EDPB (2023), p. 5.

[66] EDPB (2023), p. 5.

[67] EDPB (2023), p. 5.

subject "does not [have] a right in respect of information relating to the identity of the employees of that controller who carried out those operations under its authority and in accordance with its instructions, unless that information is essential in order to enable the data subject effectively to exercise the rights conferred on him or her by that regulation and provided that the rights and freedoms of those employees are taken into account".[68] Already in the context of the GDPR, the right of access is not generally unlimited when it comes to the protection of third persons.

3.5.2 (No) Limit of Abusive Assertion of the Right of Access

In principle, a data controller can refuse to provide information, if the claim is made in an abusive manner. However, this exception to the duty to provide information is to be interpreted very restrictively. Such a refusal may be considered, for example, when the claim is excessively asserted or manifestly unfounded.[69] High requirements are to be set for excessiveness. Thus, the claim may indeed be asserted at regular intervals multiple times without this being a reason for refusal.[70] According to Recital 63 para. 1 GDPR, the data subject already must be able to put himself in a position to be regularly aware of the data processing and to check the lawfulness.

Furthermore, it is sometimes pointed out that the data protection right of access must not pursue objectives alien to data protection.[71] It could be argued that, if a data subject requests information about the identity of the whistleblower, it is simply to know who made the accusation against him—the person against whom he can defend himself, either justifiably or unjustifiably—rather than pursuing data protection concerns. In the end, this argument is not convincing. According to Art. 15 GDPR, no purpose can be derived in connection with the right to information.[72] The German High Court (BGH) recently referred this question to the ECJ by way of a preliminary ruling procedure in accordance with Art. 267 Treaty on the Functioning of the European Union (TFEU).[73] The decision of the ECJ in this matter is still pending. However, it is likely that a general refusal on the grounds of misuse of the claim under Art. 15 para. 1. g) GDPR will be excluded.

---

[68] ECJ Judg. of 22.6.2023—C-579/21, ECLI:EU:C:2023:501, para. 83.

[69] See Art. 12 para. 5 sentence 3 GDPR.

[70] German Federal Court (BGH), Judg. of 15.6.2021—VI ZR 576/19, para. 29.

[71] Higher Regional Court (OLG) Hamm, Judg. of 3.5.2023–20 U 146/22 para. 58 et seq.; Regional Court (LG) Gießen Judg. of 11.1.2023–2 O 178/22.

[72] Cf. also Berlin Commissioner for Data Protection and Information Security, Annual Report 2022, see: https://www.datenschutz-berlin.de/jahresbericht-2022 (last accessed: 14.9.2024), p. 87 et seq.

[73] German Federal Court (BGH), Dec. of 29.3.2022—VI ZR 1352/20.

3.5.3 *Limit of Legitimate Interests of the Whistleblower*

The disclosure of the name within the framework of a right to information itself constitutes a data processing within the meaning of Art. 4 No. 2 GDPR, for which a legal basis, within the meaning of Art. 6 para. 1 GDPR, must be given. In the absence of consent, data processing on the basis of legitimate interest is primarily considered in the meaning of Art. 6 para. 1 subpara. 1. f) GDPR. In principle, a legitimate interest can be any legal, economic or ideal interest of the processor or a third party.[74] Specifically, in this context, the interest of the whistleblower in preserving the confidentiality of his identity and the interest of the person concerned, the data subject, in learning the origin of his data must be weighed against each other. According to the wording of Art. 6 para. 1 subpara. 1. f) GDPR, a predominance of whistleblower protection must be particularly demonstrated.

Especially against the background of the principle of confidentiality according to Art. 16 Whistleblower Protection Directive and its foundation in the fundamental and human rights to freedom of expression, the question arises whether a tip from an informant is generally classified as requiring confidentiality. Correctly, the need for confidentiality does not arise already from the existence of a whistleblower system. A general tendency in favour of the whistleblower cannot be invoked simply because the person concerned has the right under Art. 15 para. 1. g) GDPR as well as the fundamental right to data protection from Art. 8 EU Charter of Fundamental Rights. To answer the question of the need for confidentiality of the whistleblower's identity vis-à-vis the right to information, an individual, case-by-case assessment is required; an adequate decision can only be made this way in each specific case.

When an individual case assessment has to be made, Art. 6 para. 1 subpara. 1. f) GDPR regulates the criterion that must be taken into account in the assessment. To deny the right to information the legitimate interests of the whistleblower must outweigh the interest in information. It is not sufficient if the interest in information and the interest in confidentiality have the same weight.

Voices in the literature generally set strict requirements for whistleblower protection in the interest assessment.[75] This means that, in individual cases, not only must an abstract interest exist, but also concrete facts must be present that require confidentiality.[76] A confidentiality assurance should not fundamentally establish an obligation of confidentiality but it, too, is subject to an individual case assessment.[77]

---

[74] Albers, Veit (2023), Art. 15 GDPR Para. 68; Cf. Lachapelle (2021), p. 137 et seq.

[75] Cf. Lapp (2022), Sec. 29 para. 17; Herbst (2020), Sec. 29 para. 7 et seq.; Mallmann (2011), Sec. 19 para. 101.

[76] Cf. Mallmann (2011), Sec. 19 para. 101.

[77] Cf. Panzer-Heemeier (2023), para. 24; Altenbach, Dierkes, (2020), p. 126; Herbst (2020), Sec. 29 para. 7; Mallmann (2011), Sec. 19 para. 102.

In the context of balancing interests, it is disputed which fundamentally legitimate interests in confidentiality are of such special weight. One view demands that only those interests, the confidentiality of which, aims to avert imminent dangers to life, health or freedom of third parties have special weight and only then would there be an obligation of confidentiality.[78] Another view sees such dangers as sufficient, but not as a necessary criterion.[79]

Which interest ultimately prevails requires a more detailed examination in individual cases. The following cases taken from Germany will show some of the existing arguments in this context.

3.5.3.1 Case of German Labour Court (LAG) Baden-Württemberg, Judgement of 20 December 2018

The subject matter underlying the labour court's decision[80] concerns a former employee of a large German car manufacturer, who, among other disputes, also asserted a claim for information about performance and behavioural data related to him and stored by his employer. The Labour Court ruled in this context that a data protection right to information is not unlimited, but can be restricted under—albeit narrow—conditions, even if the possibilities for restriction did not apply in this case.

The court particularly addressed the question of whether there are overriding interests of a third party for which some information must be kept a secret, thereby limiting the right to information. It found that the mere existence of a reason for confidentiality does not per se lead to the limitation of the right to information. The withholding of certain information only applies strictly to the part for which there is actually an interest in confidentiality. In addition, a balance must be struck between the interest in information and the interest in confidentiality which takes into account the principle of proportionality.[81] Thus, in the court's view, it cannot be ruled out that the provision of information affects legitimate interests of the employer. Such a legitimate interest can also consist of the employer assuring confidentiality to whistleblowers in the scope of clarification of internal misconduct.[82] But even such protection for whistleblowers can, in individual cases, be subordinate to the interests in information. According to the court, this can be the case particularly when the whistleblower recklessly or against better knowledge provides the employer with false information. In such a case, the interest in information can have a predominant weight due to the increased need for protection.

---

[78] Cf. Herbst (2020), Sec. 29 para. 10.

[79] Cf. Lapp (2022), Sec. 29 para. 17.

[80] German Higher Regional Labour Court (LAG) Baden-Württemberg Judg. of 20.12.2018–17 Sa 11/18.

[81] German Higher Regional Labour Court (LAG) Baden-Württemberg Judg. of 20.12.2018–17 Sa 11/18, para. 229.

[82] German Higher Regional Labour Court (LAG) Baden-Württemberg Judg. of 20.12.2018–17 Sa 11/18, para. 229.

In this specific case, the court lacked a detailed justification of such confidentiality interests. The employer referred merely in general terms to whistleblower protection and to the fact that it relied on unconditional whistleblower protection. According to the court, these statements were too general and could not support a case-by-case assessment. The employer, as the defendant of the claim, was also responsible for providing evidence to prove these reasons. To clarify, the court stated that it would have been sufficient, but also necessary, to specifically explain which exact information the predominant legitimate interest in confidentiality they wished to refer to, particularly regarding the facts, incident or topic in temporal and spatial limitation as well as the acting persons. Only then would the chamber have been able to make the necessary case-by-case assessment.

3.5.3.2 Case of German Federal Court (BGH), Judgment of 22 February 2022

In the case of the tenant who alerted the landlord to the alleged vermin and odour nuisance and the affected tenant who then wanted to know the name of the whistleblower, the BGH based its decision largely on the accuracy of the information in the context of the balancing of interests. The appellate court OLG Stuttgart still denied the disclosure of the name, as this would have contradicted the data protection interests of the person giving the hint. The OLG Stuttgart emphasised the ratio from Recital 63 sentences 5, 6 DSGVO, that a balancing of interests must take place and the right to information should not be denied prematurely.[83] Similarly, the data protection interests of the whistleblower and those of the person seeking information initially stand against each other. Since the co-tenants did not show any signs that they acted against better knowledge, they should have had the opportunity to complain to the landlord about alleged grievances in the house.[84] This was the only way that the landlord could gather information on the matter and, if necessary, remedy the situation. As long as the information was factual, a tenant should expect that his information was used appropriately and treated as confidentially as possible. If the landlord were to pass on the names of the whistleblowers directly, no one would approach him anymore to report grievances within the house. It is fair to note that this case only occurred once.

At this point, the BGH emphasised the weighting provided by the legislature. According to this measure, the interests in confidentiality must prevail.[85] However, the BGH also pointed out the underlying EU law interests, particularly according to Art. 7 and 8 EU Charter of Fundamental Rights protecting the rights to privacy and

[83] German Federal Court (BGH) Judg. of 22.2.2022—VI ZR 14/21, para. 9.

[84] German Federal Court (BGH) Judg. of 22.2.2022—VI ZR 14/21, para. 9.

[85] German Federal Court (BGH) Judg. of 22.2.2022—VI ZR 14/21, para. 19.

data protection. Accordingly, per Recital 63 sentence 5 of the GDPR, the rights and freedoms of other persons should not be impaired. After all, both sides could invoke the protection of their personal data. Therefore, the disclosure of the name must have been based on a legal basis within the meaning of Art. 6 para. 1 GDPR. In the absence of consent, only Art. 6 para. 1 subpara. 1. f) GDPR is applicable. In the balancing of interests after considering the weighting, the BGH came to the conclusion that the interests of the whistleblower do not prevail.

In the balancing, it should be noted that the confidentiality interest of the whistleblower regularly recedes when he or she knowingly or negligently provides incorrect information.[86] According to the German Federal Court, it depends on the individual case whether the emphasis is on an objective or subjective correctness of the hint. For example, to ensure the effectiveness of crime fighting, an authority may refuse to provide information even if the hint was objectively incorrect.

At the same time, the data subject should have a legitimate interest in an injunction based on tort law in cases of such accusations as might potentially violate his general personal rights. An objectively incorrect factual assertion should suffice to affirm the right to information, regardless of the subjective incorrectness on the part of the informant.

The German Federal Court must be pragmatic in this respect. If it were also a matter of establishing fault, the company as the opponent of the right to information might have to carry out comprehensive quasi-criminal investigations. This hardly would be realistic or feasible. In this respect, it is conceded that the German Federal Court did not take into account the subjective side of the informant in the weighing process.

This is all the more true as the German Federal Court saw the burden of presentation and proof for the weighing with the controller.[87] According to the German Federal Court, it was up to the controller to provide concrete facts to justify the informant's overriding interest in his secrecy so the court did not have to rely on assumptions.

In this case, the German Federal Court therefore affirmed the right to information. This was the only way for the person concerned to "tackle the mistakes at the root".[88] From the perspective of effective informant protection, this may be surprising. Thus, the German Federal Court also had to withstand criticism that no one would use the informant system anymore if the weighing of interests was conducted this way. The court countered these accusations by holding that one could always act as an informant anonymously. With this argument, though, the German Federal Court overlooked the fact that an anonymous informant system can potentially be more prone to abuse.[89] According to Art. 6 para. 2 Whistleblower Protection Directive, member states may indeed set up anonymous whistleblower

[86] German Federal Court (BGH) Judg. of 22.2.2022—VI ZR 14/21, para. 31.
[87] German Federal Court (BGH) Judg. of 22.2.2022—VI ZR 14/21, para. 33.
[88] German Federal Court (BGH) Judg. of 22.2.2022—VI ZR 14/21, para. 37.
[89] Schmolke (2019), p. 897.

offices. In these cases, such hints generally would have to be followed up. However, there is no obligation to set up reporting points for anonymous reports according to Art. 6 para. 2 Whistleblower Protection Directive. Therefore, ultimately, this argument is not convincing. However, there is agreement with the opinion of the German Federal Court insofar as this interpretation takes into account the statutory wording and in particular the weighting given by the legislature.

3.5.4 Limit of a Statutory Claim, Art. 6 para. 1 subpara. 1. C) GDPR

Another potential legal basis for disclosing the identity of the whistleblower to the data subject claiming the right to access is Art. 6 para. 1 subpara. 1. c) GDPR, provided that the processing serves to fulfil a legal obligation of the controller. The decisive factor for this legal basis is an obligation on the basis of objective law. Therefore, the applicable law must impose the processing on the controller.[90] Furthermore, the statutory obligation must specifically refer to data processing.[91] Such an obligation is likely to arise from Art. 15 para. 1. g) GDPR.[92]

However, seeking justification from Art. 6 para. 1 subpara. 1. c) GDPR is circular. Starting with the right to information under Art. 15 para. 1. g) GDPR, the question arises whether it is justifiable under data protection law to disclose the identity of the whistleblower. If the right to information under Art. 15 para. 1. g) GDPR itself is used as a legal basis, this would mean that, in these cases, no legal basis must be given. This does not sufficiently respect the rights and freedoms of the person affected by the disclosure, namely the whistleblower, as provided in Art. 15 para. 4 GDPR (by analogy).

Some also mention the legal basis of Art. 6 para. 1 subpara. 1. c) GDPR in conjunction with an obligation out of the Whistleblower Protection Directive.[93] For example, Art. 17 of the Whistleblower Protection Directive could be considered. However, Art. 17 Whistleblower Protection Directive merely states that personal data are processed in the course of handling reports. Thus, Art. 17 Whistleblower Protection Directive is not suitable as a legal basis. Also the general norms, such as those on reporting offices like Art. 7 et seq. Whistleblower Protection Directive, are not sufficient, as they do not require specific data processing; they only describe general duties.

As such, the legal basis from Art. 6 para. 1 subpara. 1. f) GDPR is likely to be the sole relevant one.

---

[90] Frenzel (2021), Art. 6 para. 16.

[91] Buchner, Petri (2020), Art. 6 para. 76.

[92] Paal, Nikol (2022), p. 467.

[93] Nikol (2023), p. 352.

3.5.5 Contractual Limitation of the Right of Access

A possible limitation could arise from a context-based interpretation of Art. 15 para. 1. g) GDPR. In the aforementioned rental case[94] the tenant justified his appeal with the argument that the refusal of the right to information neither complied with the legal requirements of the GDPR nor the principle of good faith.[95]

Accordingly, one could argue that the scope of the claim could be variable based on the underlying legal relationship. Dogmatically, such an interpretation could be achieved by means of a teleological extension. In this way, contract-typical elements, such as domestic peace in the context of a residential lease, could be taken into account.

However, such a typifying possibility ultimately must be rejected. The data protection right to information is, in itself, already neutral and serves solely to assert the right to data protection under Art. 8 of the EU Charter of Fundamental Rights. As already explained above, another purpose pursued by the data subject is generally irrelevant, as it is solely about the data subject being able to assess the processing of his data. Then, however, the right to information cannot be dependent upon certain contractual obligations. Therefore, such a contract-typical restriction of the right to information must be excluded.

3.5.6 Developments From the Practice of the Authorities

Discussions on the whistleblower protection from the perspective of the data protection authorities or expert bodies go back, in part, for quite a while. The following overview sheds light on the general views, though they have significantly changed over the years. This development actually reflects the societal changes and adoption of new legal frameworks such as the Whistleblower Protection Directive.

Whereas the United States of America implemented a law in 2002 that allows whistleblowing in certain cases, states in the EU were not as advanced. Section 301 of the Sarbanes-Oxley Act of 2002 (SOX) created the obligation for public companies to establish procedures for whistleblowing channels in specific cases, especially in the context of audits. Accordingly, many multinational corporations complied with such obligations and installed mechanisms for confidential and anonymous reporting.[96] In May 2005, the Commission Nationale de l'Informatique et des Libertés (CNIL)—the competent data protection authority in France—prohibited the implementation of this kind of whistleblower

[94] German Federal Court (BGH) Judgement of 22.2.2022—VI ZR 14/21.

[95] German Federal Court (BGH) Judgement of 22.2.2022—VI ZR 14/21, para. 15.

[96] Freyer et al. (2009).

mechanism based on the SOX. The requests were submitted by McDonald's and Exide Technologies.[97] The CNIL was very cautious and critical about whistleblowing mechanisms, their stance derived from the old-fashioned point of view that whistleblowers were only "disloyal troublemakers".[98] According to the decisions, the mechanisms were not in line with French privacy laws because the mechanisms might deny individuals the right to obtain information on the nature of the allegations as well as the chance to adequately defend themselves.[99] In the following year, the Dutch Data Protection Board actually followed the French opinion and adopted a comparable statement.[100]

Shortly afterwards, the EU's Article 29 Data Protection Working Party issued an opinion that already introduced some change. The Article 29 Data Protection Working Party is an independent European advisory body on data protection and privacy and the predecessor of the current European Data Protection Board (EDPB). It adopted its Opinion 1/2006 on the application of EU data protection rules to internal whistleblowing schemes in the fields of accounting, internal accounting controls, auditing matters, fight against bribery, banking and financial crime on 1 February 2006.[101] This opinion, although non-binding in nature, dealt with the legitimacy of the whistleblowing schemes and explained i.a. the rights of the accused person. It first recalled the predecessor of Art. 15 para. 1 g) GDPR, namely that individuals are to be informed when personal data are collected from a third party and not from them directly.[102] The Working Group pointed out: "The person accused in a whistleblower's report shall be informed by the person in charge of the [whistleblowing] scheme as soon as practicably possible after the data concerning them are recorded."[103] Nevertheless, it equally stressed that the decision if and how far the accused person is to be informed must be assessed on a case-by-case basis. As to the confidentiality of the identity of the whistleblower, the Working Party stated that: "Under no circumstances can the person accused in a whistleblower's report obtain information about the identity of the whistleblower from the scheme on the basis of the accused person's right of access, except where the whistleblower maliciously makes a false statement. Otherwise, the whistleblower's confidentiality should always be guaranteed."[104]

[97] McDonald's CNIL Délibération No 2005–110; CEAC/Exide Technologies CNIL Délibération No 2005–111 of 26.5.2005.

[98] Lewis 2011, p. 2.

[99] McDonald's CNIL Délibération No 2005–110; CEAC/Exide Technologies CNIL Délibération No 2005–111 of 26.5.2005.

[100] Dutch Data Protection Authority, Whistle blowing—Opinion Dutch DPA—January 2006.

[101] Article 29 Data Protection Working Party, Opinion 1/2006 of 1.2.2006, 00195/06/EN.

[102] Article 29 Data Protection Working Party, Opinion 1/2006 of 1.2.2006, 00195/06/EN, p. 13 et seq.

[103] Article 29 Data Protection Working Party, Opinion 1/2006 of 1.2.2006, 00195/06/EN, p. 13.

[104] Article 29 Data Protection Working Party, Opinion 1/2006 of 1.2.2006, 00195/06/EN, p. 14.

The initial skepticism of the CNIL now has turned into a rather proactive support for whistleblower protection. The latest opinion paper by the CNIL, on the matter of whistleblower protection of 2023, addresses various aspects of whistleblowing channels such as the rightful legitimate basis under GDPR law. It also mentions, with regard to the relevant French law for whistleblower protection, that when a report is issued in good faith, the organizations must generally guarantee the confidentiality of the whistleblower's identity.[105] Comparable views can be found in statements or guidelines from other data protection authorities in the EU.[106]

After all, most of the time, the statements simply highlight the importance of the right of access on the one hand and the confidentiality of the whistleblower's identity on the other hand. They do not, however, answer the question of how to balance both interests in specific situations in the relevant phases of the internal investigations. Therefore, balancing both interests requires a closer look as will be taken in the following chapter.

3.6 Conclusion

After highlighting key aspects of the whistleblower protection, it is clear that a sincere informant who reports a possible violation of rules in his company via a designated channel, generally enjoys protection of his identity. With his report, he not only protects himself, but often also his employer, his colleagues, the economy in general and even the rule of law as a whole. Exceptions may only apply in the case of improper motives of the whistleblower or in the case of intentionally dishonest reports.

The analysis of the right of access leads to the conclusion that, such right under data protection law is an essential tool for the data subject to get an overview of the next necessary steps and in particular whether and to what extent he wants to take action against the whistleblower. At the same time, the claim potentially may be an effective tool to undermine the whistleblower protection. The right of access under Art. 15 para. 1. g) GDPR is a sharp sword, which in principle prevails with very minimal room for opposition. Employers who are faced with a claim to the right to information under Art. 15 para. 1. g) GDPR, for the purpose of inquiring about the identity of the whistleblower, must weigh extensively between the conflicting interests. Therefore, the question becomes how such a balance may be achieved.

---

105 CNIL (2023), para. 23.

106 Cf. e.g. Italian Data Protection Authority, Newsletter on the need to protect the identity of the whistleblower (2021).

References

Academic Articles and Contributions

Albers MV, Raoul-Darius, Heinrich Amadeus W, Beck's BS (2023) Online commentary data protection law, 45th edn

Altenbach T, Dierkes, Kevin (2020) EU Whistleblowing directive and GDPR. Corporate Compliance J, 126

Bienemann L (2022) In Sydow G, Marsch N (eds) European general data protection regulation. 3rd edn. GDPR

Bishop-Monroe R, Cockrell SR, Harrison BM. Di Paolo M, Gloria J (2021) Thank you whistleblower! How organizations can cultivate whistleblower activity to enhance business success. Organ Dyn, 50:1

Bräutigam P, Schmidt-Wudy F (2015) The planned right of access and disclosure of the data subject according to Art. 15 of the EU General data protection regulation. Comput Law, 56

Bruns P (2025) In: Beck-online GROSSKOMMENTAR Labour Law, German Whistleblower Protection Act, Rolfs C, Giesen R, Udsching P, Meßling M (eds), 75th edn

Buchner B, Petri T (2020) In: Kühling J, Buchner B (eds) GDPR/FDPA, 3rd edn

Dilling J (2020) Interne Ermittlungen im Spannungsfeld zwischen Unternehmensstrafrecht und Whistleblowing. J Corporate Compliance CCZ, 132

Dix A (2019) In: GDPR general data protection regulation, Spiecker gen. Döhmann I, Papakonstantinou V, Hornung G, De Hert P (eds), 1st edn

Dix A (2023) In: GDPR General Data Protection Regulation, Spiecker gen. Döhmann I, Papakonstantinou V, Hornung G, De Hert P (eds), 1st edn

Dendorfer-Ditges R (2025) In: Münchener Anwaltshandbuch Arbeitsrecht, Moll W, Eckhoff F, Reufels M (eds), 6th edn

Dzida B, Granetzny T (2020) Die neue EU-Whistleblowing-Richtlinie und ihre Auswirkungen auf Unternehmen. Neue Zeitschrift Für Arbeitsrecht, 1201

Franck L (2022) In: Gola P, Dirk H (eds) General data protection regulation – federal Data Protection Act, 3rd edn

Freyer, Dana H, DiBianco G, Servan-Schreiber P, Horbach M, Ashley KD (2009) Whistleblower programs: challenges for multinational companies. Available at: https://www.skadden.com/-/media/Files/Publications/2009/03/Publications1719_0.pdf?sc_lang=en

Frenzel EM (2021) In Paal B, Pauly D (eds) General data protection regulation, Federal data protection act, 3rd edn

Gräber T, NoldenChristine (2021) In Paal B, Pauly D (eds) General Data Protection Regulation Federal Data Protection Act, 3rd edn

Grabitz E, Hilf M (2009) The Law of the European Union, 38th edn. Directive (EEC) 95/46

Grobys I, Panzer-Heemeier A (2023) Keyword commentary employment law, 4th Edition

Herbst T (2020) In: Kühling J, Buchner B (eds) GDPR/FDPA, 3rd edn

Kämmerer, Jan-Philip/Redder Jan-Philip (2025) Beck-online GROSSKOMMENTAR German Whistleblower Protection Act. In: Schubert C, Kämmerer JA, Veil R (eds), Edition

Lachapelle A (2021) Whistleblowing: threat or Safeguard for Data Protection in the Digital Era? in Deep diving into data protection: 1979-2019: celebrating 40 years of research on privacy data protection at the CRIDS. Collection du CRIDS. Larcier, Bruxelles, 51, 129–148

Lapp T (2022) In: Peter G, Dirk H (eds) General data protection regulation – federal Data Protection Act, 3rd edn

Lewis D (2011) Whistleblowing and data protection principles: is the road to reconciliation really that rocky? Euro J Law Technol 2:1

Liedke B (2014) Big data – small information: does the data protection right to information need to be reformed? Communication & Law, 714

Mallmann O (2011) In: Spiros simitis, federal data protection act, 7th edn

Maschmann F (2021) Der Arbeitgeber als Verantwortlicher für den Datenschutz im Betriebsratsbüro (§ 79 a BetrVG)?, Neue Zeitschrift Für Arbeitsrecht, 834
Mengel A (2023) Compliance und Arbeitsrecht, 2nd edn
Musiol P (2024) Datenschutzrechtliche Verantwortlichkeit und Auskunftsrechte des Hinweisgebers – ein Perspektivwechsel, CCZ
Nikol D (2023) On the tension between whistleblower protection and data protection law, 9 Compliance Advisor, 352
Paal B (2021) In Paal B, Pauly D (eds) General data protection regulation Federal Data Protection Act, 3rd edn
Paal B, Nikol D (2022) On the identification of whistleblowers in the tension between the Whistleblower Protection Act, Whistleblowing Directive and General Data Protection Regulation. Compliance Advisor, 466
Papakonstantinou V, De Hert P (2023) In: Dix A (ed) Spiecker Gen. Döhmann I, Papakonstantinou V, Hornung G, De Hert P (eds) GDPR General Data Protection Regulation, 1st edn
Reufels MJ, Soltysiak L (2023) Das neue Whistleblowing-Recht, 1st edn
Schmidt-Wudy F (2023) In Heinrich WA, Brinck S, Beck's Online Commentary Data Protection Law, 45th edn
Schmolke U (2019) Whistleblowing als Regelungsaufgabe, Zeitschrift Für Unternehmens- Und Gesellschaftsrecht, 876
Stollhoff S (2020) In: Eßer M, Kramer P, Lewinski K (eds) GDPR/FDPA, 7th edn

Court Decisions

ECJ Judg. of 11.4.2024 – c-741/21, ECLI:EU:C:2024:288
ECJ Judg. of 12.1.2023 – c-154/21 ECLI:EU:C:2023:3
ECJ Judg. of 4.5.2023 – c-487/21, ECLI:EU:C:2023:369
ECJ, Judg. of 30.3.2023 – c-34/21, ECLI:EU:C:2023:270
ECJ Judg. of 22.6.2023 – c-579/21, ECLI:EU:C:2023:501
ECJ, Judg. of 7.3.2024 – C-604/22, ECLI:EU:C:2024:214
ECJ Judg. of 7.3.2024 – c-740/22, ECLI:EU:C:2024:216
ECJ, Judg. of 20.12.2017 – c-434/16, ECLI:EU:C:2017:994
ECJ, Judg. of 19.10.2016 – c-582/14, ECLI:EU:C:2017:563
ECJ Judg. of 13.5.2014 – c-131/12, ECLI:EU:C:2013:424
ECJ Judg. of 10.7.2018 – c-25/17, ECLI:EU:C:2018:551
ECJ Judg. of 11.1.2024 – c-231/22, ECLI:EU:C:2024:7
ECJ Ruling of 27.5.2024 – C-312/23, Addiko Bank
Federal Labour Court (BAG), Judg. of 16.12.2021 – 2 AZR 235/21, also in: NZA 2022, 362
German Federal Court (BGH), Dec. of 29 3 2022 – VI ZR 1352/20
German Federal Court (BGH), Judg of 15 6 2021 – VI ZR 576/19
German Federal Court (BGH), Judg of 22 2 2022 – VI ZR 14/21
Higher Regional Court (OLG) Hamm, Judg. of 3.5 2023 20 U 146/22
Higher Regional Court (OLG) Stuttgart, Judg. of 10.12.2020 13 U 278/20
Regional Court (LG) Gießen Judg. of 11.1.2023 – 2 O 178/22
Regional Labour Court (LAG) Baden-Württemberg, Judg. of 20.12.2018 – 17 Sa 11/18

Official Documents and Treaties

Article 29 Working Party Opinion 4/2007 on the concept of personal data, Wp 136, 20.06. 2007

Berlin Commissioner for Data Protection and Information Security, Annual Report 2022, see: https://www.datenschutz-berlin.de/jahresbericht-2022

Commission Nationale de l'Informatique et des Libertés (CNIL), Référentiel relative aux traitements de données à caractère personnel destinés à la mise en œuvre d'un dispositif d'alterte of 6, 6, 2023

Commission Nationale de l'Informatique et des Libertés (CNIL), Délibération No 2005-111 of 26.5.2005, CEAC/Exide Technologies

Commission Nationale de l'Informatique et des Libertés (CNIL), Délibération No 2005-110 of 26.5.2005, McDonald's

Dutch Data Protection Authority, Whistle blowing – opinion Dutch DPA – January 2006

European Data Protection Board (EDPB), Guidelines on data subject rights – right of Access, March 2023

European Data Protection Board (EDPB), Guidelines on the concepts of controller and processor in the GDPR, March 2023

European Data Protection Board (EDPB), Guidelines on processing personal information within a whistleblowing procedure, December 2019

German Parliament Print Document 20/3442

International Bar Association, Whistleblower Protections: a Guide, April 2018

Italian Data Protection Authority, Newsletter on the need to protect the identity of the whistleblower, August 2021

Official Documents and Treaties

Council of Europe, Convention 108+, Convention for the protection of individuals with regard to the processing of personal data

Whistleblowing Report 2021, available at: https://www.humanrights.ch/cms/upload/pdf/2021/211018_Whistleblowing_report_2021_DE_final.pdf

Chapter 4
Synthesizing the Confidentiality of Whistleblowers and the Right of Access

Based on the above-mentioned dilemma regarding the whistleblower's protection under EU and the Council of Europe law on the one hand and the data protection right of access under EU law on the other hand, the question arises under what conditions is an employer obliged in an individual case to provide the desired information to the data subject and to what extent must the employer protect the confidentiality of the whistleblower's identity. The fact that these two rights may directly clash has already been foreseen by the legislator of the Whistleblower Protection Directive. In Recital 84 Whistleblower Protection Directive, it reads in particular that it should be ensured "that this Directive is effective, including, where necessary, by restricting, by legislative measures, the exercise of certain data protection rights of persons concerned [. . .] to the extent, and as long as, necessary to prevent and address attempts to hinder reporting or to impede, frustrate or slow down follow-up, in particular investigations, or attempts to find out the identity of the reporting persons".[1]

This question does not only focus on whether or not to hand over the whistleblower's name or identity, but also handing over any kind of information that may not contain the whistleblower's full name, but from which the affected person may derive the whistleblower's identity nevertheless, for instance based on specific knowledge presented in the report or circumstances that lead to the conclusion of only one single individual as the whistleblower. Unless all this information is protected, the protection of the whistleblower is void. If the whistleblower falls under the protective mechanism of the legal regime, then his or her identity should be held confidential and no indicative information may be disclosed.

According to Art. 15 para 1. g) GDPR, the person concerned has a right of access to i.a. the origin of his or her data against the employer as controller, which

[1] Recital 84 Whistleblower Protection Directive.

S. Koloßa, *Whistleblower Protection and the Right of Access*, SpringerBriefs in Law,
https://doi.org/10.1007/978-3-032-04817-2_4

is a right to information about the identity of the whistleblower. Art. 16 para. 1 Whistleblower Protection Directive establishes that the identity of the whistleblower and all information from which the identity can be derived, must be protected. Specifically, Art. 16 para. 2 Whistleblower Protection Directive states that the identity may only be disclosed if this is a legally necessary duty and also a proportional duty with regard to the preservation of the defence rights of the person concerned. As demonstrated above, a corresponding protection of the identity of the whistleblower results from Art. 10 ECHR.

The fact, that the right of access under Art. 15 GDPR is not absolute and may generally be balanced against the rights under the Whistleblower Protection Directive, is already explicitly foreseen by the GDPR. Art. 23 para. 1. i) GDPR prescribes that the EU as well as any Member State's domestic law may restrict the right of access under Art. 15 GDPR, as long as the restriction respects the essence of the fundamental rights and freedoms of the data subject, while the restriction is a necessary and proportionate measure in a democratic society. The Whistleblower Protection Directive as well as the national laws on whistleblower protection may fall under this exemption.[2] One may also invoke the exception of Art. 23 para. 1. e) GDPR under which restrictions are allowed if the legal acts pursue other important objectives of general public interest of the EU or of a Member State, in particular an important economic or financial interest of the EU or of a Member State, including monetary, budgetary and taxation matters, public health and social security.[3]

The fact that the case law of the ECtHR and the obligations from the ECHR primarily address the contracting states and not directly to private actors, does not make the decisions of the ECtHR irrelevant for the balance in the concrete situation of an employer. Several voices advocate for at least an indirect third-party effect of the human rights obligations under the ECHR.[4] Indirect third-party effect means that private individuals are not directly bound by the human rights enshrined in the ECHR, but they can expect and rely on a convention-compliant interpretation of the national laws.[5] The ECtHR tends to take a more critical stance on this, but ultimately also argues that it is up to the positive obligations of a state to ensure the compliance with the rights and freedoms stipulated by the ECHR.[6] Additionally, the ECHR has a varying status in national member states' legislation. In some states such as Germany or Italy, the ECHR has the status of a simple law, but it still

[2] Cf. also Trojsi, The confirmed, indeed reinforced, Centrality of the GDPR for the Protection of Workers' Personal Rights in the light of subsequent EU Legislative Acts, 2 Italian Labour Law e-Journal 17 (2024), p. 358.

[3] Cf. also Trojsi, The confirmed, indeed reinforced, Centrality of the GDPR for the Protection of Workers' Personal Rights in the light of subsequent EU Legislative Acts, 2 Italian Labour Law e-Journal 17 (2024), p. 358.

[4] Nettesheim (2023), Art. 1, para. 19; Krieger (2022), Chap. 6 para. 82.

[5] Schubert (2024), Art. 1 para. 42.

[6] See only ECtHR Judg. of 5.9.2017–61,496/08, Barbulescu against Romania, para. 109, 111.

has a special force that exceeds the normal constitutional discipline of international norms.[7] Due to the international law friendliness of the German Basic Law, there is an obligation to also consider the jurisprudence of the ECtHR. In other states such as Austria and the Netherlands, the ECHR is directly awarded constitutional rank.[8] States like France, Belgium, Spain, and Portugal attribute a super-legislative ranking to the ECHR.[9] Even though the EU itself is still not bound by the ECHR, all 27 EU member states are members of the ECHR, so the ECHR and the decisions of the ECtHR have to be taken into account.[10] Therefore, even though the obligations of the ECHR primarily address the states and especially the national legislator, the rights and freedoms under the ECHR including the decisions of the ECtHR on whistleblower protection are included into the following synthesis and balanced with the framework of the right of access to the origins of the personal data under Art. 15 para. 1. g) GDPR.

The specific legal balancing question is to be posed within the framework of the data protection law, as the information about the identity of the whistleblower constitutes a processing of personal data of the whistleblower and requires a justification in the sense of Art. 4 No. 2 GDPR, for which a legal basis according to Art. 6 para. 1 GDPR is necessary. The justifications from Art. 6 para. 1 GDPR in turn protect the rights of the whistleblower (third party) in the sense of Art. 15 para. 4 GDPR. In other words, the suspected person may ask for the personal data of the whistleblower under the right of access, but providing that data is not to be measured (only) within the right of access; it does constitute a separate personal data processing which needs to be justified. The aim is nevertheless "[t]he effective protection of the confidentiality of the identity of reporting persons [. . .] for the protection of the rights and freedoms of others, in particular those of the reporting person".[11]

One legal basis for handing over the requested information on the identity of the whistleblower under data protection law is the legitimate interest of the data subject, Art. 6 para. 1 subpara. 1. f) GDPR. The basis of a legitimate interest follows a balancing test including three questions to answer: Does the handing over of the data constitute an interest that is legitimate in the meaning of the GDPR? Is it necessary to hand over the data on the whistleblower in order to realize the legitimate interest? Are the interests of the data subject overridden by the interests or fundamental rights and freedoms of the whistleblower?

As shown above, asking for the identity of the whistleblower as the source of personal data on the data subject constitutes a legitimate interest, as this is part of the right to access under Art. 15 para. 1 g) GDPR. Furthermore, it is necessary to process the whistleblower's personal data in order to comply with the request. The essential question requiring the most scrutiny is balancing the interests of the

[7] Martinico (2012), p. 404.

[8] Martinico (2012), p. 404.

[9] Martinico (2012), p. 404.

[10] Mohn (2022), p. 1165.

[11] See Recital 84 Whistleblower Protection Directive.

persons involved. As a principle in the context of balancing such interests, Art. 6 para. 1 subpara. 1. f) GDPR establishes a tendency in favour of the third party, i.e. the suspected person here. The claim is only to be denied if the interests of the whistleblower in keeping their data confidential actually outweighs the data subject's interest. If both interests are equally present, the interest in information takes precedence over the interest in secrecy. The following balancing therefore needs to work when the interests of the whistleblower outweighs the interest in information of the person concerned.

Another legal basis for providing the information is the right of access itself (Art. 15 GDPR), which may be taken as a statutory claim under Art. 6 para. 1 subpara. 1. c) GDPR. The GDPR allows for a data processing if such processing is required by law. Nevertheless, this would still not be a yes or no question as the right to access also foresees a balancing test. Then the decision whether or not to deny access to the requested information would depend on the balancing of interests within the limits of the right of access, namely Art. 15 para. 4 GDPR. The actual balancing of the interests involved largely resembles the one within Art. 6 para. 1 subpara. 1. f) GDPR. The right to obtain the information shall not adversely affect the rights and freedoms of the whistleblower. Hence, just like with the previous legal basis, there is a tendency towards providing the information unless there is a preponderant interest of the whistleblower's protection. This in fact contradicts the above-mentioned tendency towards predominantly protecting the whistleblower's identity and keep it confidential.

As can be seen from the explanations, the accuracy of the reported information is crucial (**see under 4.1.**). The intention of the whistleblower is of relevance, regardless of the accuracy of the report (**see under 4.2.**). The importance of the matter could also play a role in the balancing, especially with regard to its importance for society (**see under 4.3.**). The employer, who is faced with the duty to balance conflicting interests, must also convince himself of the accuracy of the reported information, follow up on the hints and conduct an internal investigation (**see under 4.4.**). In this context, certain at least temporarily limited rights to refuse information may exist (**see under 4.5.**). In the end, these aspects shall provide the main focal points on which a decision on whether or not to provide access to the identity of the whistleblower may be based. Due to the complexity of national supplementary statutes, the precise weight of the arguments may differ. However, the decision is in all cases primarily based on the facts in a specific case. Therefore, it is important to conduct a thorough case-by-case analysis.[12] When determining the preponderant interest in the concrete case, the established criteria for whistleblower protection are to be considered.

[12] Article 29 Working Party (2006), p. 14.

4.1 Accuracy of the Reported Information

In the context of determining the accuracy of the information, three typical situations may arise: The whistleblower knowingly or willingly makes false statements (**see under 1.1**), the whistleblower's hint is objectively correct (**see under 1.2**), the hint is objectively incorrect, but the whistleblower believed in the accuracy of the information (**see under 1.3**).

4.1.1 Whistleblower Knowingly or Willingly Makes False Statements

Overall, as outlined above, according to both the Whistleblower Protection Directive and Article 10 ECHR as well as the *Guja* criteria of the ECtHR, the whistleblower is not awarded with the full protection in any case, if he knowingly or willingly makes false statements in the report. This limitation of whistleblower protection is well justified for several reasons. First, a whistleblower who intentionally makes false claims and defames another person, is not only morally not worthy of legal whistleblower protection but actually faces criminal charges, in particular the offences of defamation or slander under the respective national legal regime.[13] If the whistleblower makes himself criminally liable through his report, he should not be granted full whistleblower protection because his actions cannot be awarded with legal protection in one branch of the law where it is condemned under another branch of the law.

A whistleblower may not only face charges for the violation of the data subject's rights, but also when disclosing secret information which are protected by the Trade Secrets Directive.[14] In a situation like the one this analysis focuses on, namely the reporting of potential misconduct through internal channels, it is hard to imagine a situation with a violation of trade secrets law without violating the rights of the data subject. Considering, the violation of the data subject's rights, that by itself would not amount to a criminal offense resulting in charges and that would only affect the data subject in a minor way, it bears the question of whether the whistleblower may claim to get to know the identity of the whistleblower. Generally, the pure violation of trade secrets may well be considered to the detriment of the whistleblower under the aspect of a type of sanction.[15] Although the protection of trade secrets is at least not primarily aimed at

[13] In the case of Germany, defamation is criminalized under Sec. 186 German Criminal Code and slander under Sec. 187 German Criminal Code.

[14] (EU) Directive 2016/943 of 8.6.2016.

[15] See Art. 16 (EU) Directive 2016/943.

protecting the affected data subject, it is already sufficient that the whistleblower acted in a way, that the law condemns. This leads once again to losing the protected status as whistleblower.

Another argument in favour of lowering the whistleblower's protection is the fact that a whistleblower's false reporting leads to the employer having to waste resources for the internal investigations to be carried out. In light of the legal principle that is known in most national laws that it is prohibited to file a report of a non-existent crime, in particular to protect the judiciary from unnecessary investigative activities, the whistleblower who reports a non-existent crime should not enjoy protection.[16] Clearly, prohibiting reporting non-existent crimes is a principle that protects the affected person as well.

After all, the data subject in order to have a claim in the meaning of the right of access under Art. 15 GDPR must be at least remotely affected by the report of the whistleblower. Then, it is justified to grant the data subject access to the relevant data on the falsely reporting whistleblower. However, this type of liability and involvement of third-party interests will not be elaborated on further at this point.

If there is a (possible) criminal liability, the affected person must be granted the right to learn who has unjustifiably violated his honour. Because then he may have claims for damages or at least for an injunction.[17] This is also part of the principle of fair trial, a principle that is enshrined in Art. 6 para. 1 ECHR as well as in Art. 22 Whistleblower Protection Directive.

However, it is crucial to note that at least according to the ECtHR, even in such cases, in which the whistleblower does not enjoy the protection of their identity and of their confidentiality, the whistleblower protection under the legal regime does not fade entirely fade, but rather the level of protection decreases.[18] This means that the whistleblower may not enjoy confidentiality against the data subject, but his or her privileges under the legal whistleblower protection regime, at least under Art. 10 ECHR, may still be available. The level of the remaining protection depends on the circumstances of the individual case. Nevertheless, such a decrease in the level of whistleblower protection in relation to the balancing of the interests in the information in question is likely to always result in the interest in information prevailing in these cases. The interest in information tends to prevail due to the legal intention that it should generally prevail and only take the back seat in exceptional cases when yielding to the interest in whistleblower protection. So if it turns out that the whistleblower has deliberately reported false information, the interest in information is likely to prevail in most cases.

---

[16] Cf. only ECtHR Judg. of 12.2.2008–14,277/04, Guja against Moldova.

[17] ECtHR Judg. of 16.02.2021–23,922/19, Gawlik against Liechtenstein.

[18] See only ECtHR Judg. of 12.2.2008–14,277/04, Guja against Moldova, para. 53.

4.1.2 *Objectively Correct Hint of the Whistleblower*

If a whistleblower reports information that is actually true, there is initially much to suggest that this person should be protected. In particular, the affected person is then likely to have no reasonable interest in taking action against the whistleblower because of possible false information. If the affected suspect wishes to reprimand the whistleblower for personal reasons like revenge, this is exactly what the whistleblower protection should protect the whistleblower from. The whistleblower protection regularly applies and outweighs the right of access. The predominantly prevailing interest in protecting the whistleblower can, however, still be subject to the interest in providing information for other reasons. For example, whistleblower protection can be omitted due to dishonest motives (**see under 2.**). It could also be omitted if the hint does not aim at an illegal act, but only at a morally reprehensible act (**see under 3.**).

4.1.3 *Good Faith in the Accuracy of Objectively Incorrect or Inaccurate Information; Whistleblower's Duty of Inquiry*

According to the principle of good faith, it is also convincing that hints, which later turn out to be incorrect, but were initially reported on reasonable grounds, also fall under whistleblower protection. At this point, however, the quality of the reported information is crucial. In particular, a whistleblower must not merely rely on his gut feeling when making a report and formulate pure suspicions, but must do everything in his power that is at the same time reasonable to confirm his suspicion.

Nevertheless, the whistleblower cannot be obliged to completely clarify the matter on his own, so to say to provide the employer with a perfectly investigated case. In practice, it will hardly be possible for a whistleblower to achieve a definitive and final clarification of the facts and at the same time provide complete proof. Since whistleblower protection is not only a right in the sense of EU law, but is also protected by human rights under Art. 10 ECHR, the whistleblower must generally be granted protection if he acted in good faith and at the same time had justified reasons from his point of view that his assumptions were correct.[19]

Noteworthy is the restrictive assessment of the ECtHR in the Gawlik case, in which the court insisted that the complainant should have carried out further checks after Mr. Gawlik came to the conclusion that there had been medical mistakes, especially after an expert opinion found Mr. Gawlik's original suspicion quite understandable.[20] Moreover, the decision is inconsistent insofar as the ECtHR

[19] See also Gerdemann, Colneric (2021), p. 207.

[20] Lühning (2023), p. 140.

pointed out the interests of the hospital in a good reputation, but at the same time justified violations of professional secrecy in the Halet case, just so that the published legal practices were rightly discussed in public. It can be assumed that there was indeed a suspicion of a criminal offence. The Federal Constitutional Court has also ruled that employees are protected from dismissal if they do not knowingly make false or reckless statements.[21] Whether whistleblower protection was actually to be denied due to the suspicion and the risk of repetition is questionable.[22]

For an employer who has to consider these aspects in his assessment, the decision is not always straightforward. In a specific individual case, it is hardly possible to determine with certainty when a suspicion was justified. One aspect that counts towards protecting the whistleblower is a lack of direct personal involvement. The more the whistleblower is distant from the reported case and the less the whistleblower may have a personal gain from the report, the more he or she is worthy of protection. Furthermore, an employer should protect the whistleblower the more he or she has reported in a purely procedural manner without much of emotional acclamations and including the reporting of other sources. In other words, if he has gone to the trouble of using another source in the attempt to justify the accusation, the whistleblower's protection is more likely to be justified.

Ultimately, a whistleblower can already reduce the risk of a false report by providing more factual information about the situation, but not drawing any legal conclusions himself.[23] The factual nature of the provided information may well be seen as a valuable criterion for the employer in favour of the whistleblower.

4.2 Intentions of the Whistleblower

Normally, it can be assumed that a whistleblower, especially if they report correct information, is primarily interested in eliminating the reported misconduct. However, in some cases, it may happen that the whistleblower primarily pursues the goal of taking revenge on another person, securing a better position for themselves in the company, or even pursuing other financial interests. Then the question arises as to whether these aspects should be taken into account. At this point, there is a discrepancy between EU law and the law of the Council of Europe. While, according to the above-mentioned case law of the ECtHR and in particular the *Guja* criteria, a whistleblower enjoys only limited protection if they primarily pursue selfish, non-material purposes, Recital 32 sentence 5 Whistleblower Protection Directive recommends that it should not matter for what reasons the whistleblower reports the information.

[21] German Constitutional Court (BVerfG) Dec. of 2.7.2001–1 BvR 2049/00.

[22] Meyer (2023), p. 267.

[23] ECtHR Judg. of 12.2.2008–14,277/04, Guja against Moldova, para. 71.

The reason for this difference lies within the different legal bases. The Whistleblower Protection Directive primarily aims to protect the reporting itself, especially with regard to effective elimination of misconduct.[24] The discrepancy can be resolved. On the one hand, this aspect from the Whistleblower Protection Directive is only found in the recitals, not in the binding operative part of the directive. On the other hand, it is formulated as a should-rule, so that there is no absolute prohibition written here to completely ignore the intention of the whistleblower. Finally, the *Guja* criteria do not provide that any motive other than the aim of eliminating misconduct automatically leads to a restriction of whistleblower protection. Rather, it should be avoided that the elimination of misconduct completely fades into the background when reporting. In practice, there are rarely clear indications of this.

Therefore, it should be sufficient for the employer in the context of the evaluation to take into account motives depending on their severity, if the motives reveal themselves at all. This can be the case if there are an excessive number of attacks on one person or if a special remuneration becomes evident. Then it is possible to conclude a dishonest motivation. The employer must take this into account in its assessment.

When balancing the interests at stake, in the presence of dominant dishonest reasons such as revenge, envy, self-promotion, the whistleblower protection is likely to retreat in favour of the interest in granting the right of access. Although the ECtHR emphasises that the protection of the person giving the hint does not completely disappear in these cases, yet they no longer enjoy the full extent.[25] Due to the basic evaluation already provided by law in Art. 6 para. 1 subpara. 1. f) GDPR, according to which the interest in whistleblower protection must significantly outweigh the interest in information in order to prevail, it is unlikely that whistleblower protection outweighs the interest in information at a reduced level. In the end, it should also be the core motivation of the whistleblower to stop the illegitimate conduct for him or her to assume the protection by the whistleblower protection law.

4.3 (Societal) Importance and Impact of the Matter

An interesting question arises with regard to the relevance or the importance and impact of the matter at the heart of the reporting, both for the parties themselves and for the general public. The ECtHR attached considerable importance to this aspect, which was particularly evident in the *Gawlik* case. There, the ECtHR justified a breach of several confidentiality obligations of the whistleblower with

[24] ECtHR Judg. of 16.2.2021–23,922/19, Gawlik against Liechtenstein.

[25] Cf. Committee of Ministers of the Council of Europe, Recommendation CM/Rec(2014)7 on the protection of whistleblowers of 30.4.2014, Principle 4 para. 41.

the interest in a public debate of a behaviour that is legal in itself.[26] Now, in relation to the question underlying this analysis, it would be easy to attach little weight to this aspect, as the ECtHR's decision was about the dissemination of information to the public, not the use of internal reporting channels. Nevertheless, the criterion of the importance of the matter for the public interest is an integral part of human rights protection according to the *Guja* criteria.

In particular, against the background of the *Gawlik* case, the employer might question the need for protection of the whistleblower if he makes statements to the detriment of the person concerned that do not relate to an illegal act. According to the Whistleblower Protection Directive, the protection of the whistleblower only applies to certain violations of EU law. The question therefore arises to what extent does the whistleblower enjoy further protection. From a human rights perspective, extended protection seems fundamentally necessary, so that a whistleblower who does not report an illegal act cannot be denied whistleblower protection.

This should not be unreasonable in the context of balancing with the interest in information. The interest in information with regard to the assertion of possible injunction or damage claims against the whistleblower should not weigh as heavily in view of the less serious accusations and the less serious defamation compared to those related to illegal acts. In this constellation, a detailed balance is therefore required. The balancing of interests must also take place in the context of society at the stage of internal reporting only.[27]

In the mentioned rental case, it was specifically about the "preservation of order and peace in the house community".[28] The German Federal Court did not recognise the securing this social peace, in order to avoid disputes or court proceedings among tenants, as an overriding interest. The employer should therefore, and by analogy also see little reason to give much weight to the impact of the underlying matter in internal company situations.

At the same time, the criterion of potential damages for the employer from the *Guja* case seems somewhat intangible from the employer's perspective. The ECtHR seems to consider the consequences of a report for the employer so that whistleblower protection also depends on the consequences for the company itself. Especially in the *Halet* case, it became clear that even legal behaviour, which a whistleblower considers to be socially debatable and brings to the public, triggers whistleblower protection. In retrospect, it could be argued that in this case the actual damage according to the ECtHR's decision was not significant. However, this result is difficult to predict from an *ex ante* perspective. In doubt, the criterion of potential damage should not serve as a reason for the employer to deny whistleblower protection.

---

[26] German Federal Court (BGH) Judg. of 22.2.2022—VI ZR 14/21 para. 9.

[27] Petri (2023), para. 166; Dendorfer-Ditges (2021), Sec. 35 para. 97.

[28] Petri (2023), para. 166; Dendorfer-Ditges (2021), Sec. 35 para. 97.

4.4 Determination of the Accuracy of the Information Through an Internal Investigation Procedure

The employer can rarely directly evaluate the above-mentioned criteria. If the employer receives indications of irregularities in the company, he is initially obliged to deal with the presented facts and initiate the necessary investigations.[29] Initially, it would likely be necessary in a first step to narrow down the specific subject of the investigation to the reported information.[30] This first step is of crucial importance for the entire investigation process and aims to make the procedure as targeted and efficient as possible. The fact that the investigation process should be as short as possible, especially in terms of time, is also of significant importance with regard to a claimed right to information, as otherwise conflicts with the generally short information period of one month according to Art. 12 para. 3 GDPR can occur. In a second step, the employer must investigate the facts through the appropriate responsible persons.[31] This investigation of the facts can be carried out with the help of the internal audit department, but also external law firms, auditors or other experts can be hired to do these tasks. Specific deadlines cannot be set due to the complexity of the possible facts.

It is important to note that the internal investigations must be carried out regardless of the assertion of a right to information. The right to information is likely to be asserted in the course of internal investigations in order to quickly ascertain the identity of the whistleblower and thus, from the perspective of the person concerned, to find out the originator of the accusations against the person concerned.

During the investigations, the question arises in particular whether there is a right of the employer to deny, at least temporarily until the completion of the investigations, the information about the identity of the whistleblower.

4.4.1 Dilatory Right to Refuse Information While Conducting an Internal Investigations

As already outlined above, case law has emphasised that a restriction on the right to information must be interpreted narrowly and only applied to those parts of the information for which it is necessary. Under no circumstances may the entire information be rejected for the protection of the whistleblower's identity.

To achieve a fair balance between the interest in information and the interest in confidentiality, the right of access could be postponed for a time, namely until the

[29] Petri (2023), Sec. 5, para. 167; Dendorfer-Ditges (2021), Sec. 35 para. 97.

[30] Wessing (2023), Sec. 147 para. 5.

[31] Wessing (2023), Sec. 147 para. 6.

completion of the internal investigations. This would be a temporary procedure and rights-preserving measure, so-called dilatory. Such a regulation is also in line with the public investigation procedures by the member states. As long as the public prosecutor's office has not noted the completion of the investigations in the files,[32] the defence counsel can be denied access to the investigation files[33] insofar as this can endanger the purpose of the investigation.

The wording of the norm suggests that such a refusal is only permissible in exceptional cases.[34] Access to the files must not be routinely denied. It is always necessary to assess whether the purpose of the investigation is actually endangered by the inspection of the files. Such a danger is considered to exist, according to the prevailing view, if there are objectively present and factually substantiated indications that the accused, upon becoming aware of the contents of the files, would interfere in the investigation proceedings in an impermissible manner.[35] Only a minority opinion does not consider a specific danger necessary.[36] The indications that speak for a refusal of inspection must not merely be of a general nature, but must rather relate to the specific circumstances in the individual case, namely the personality of the accused, the nature of the offence in question, and the nature of the investigations.

If an affected person requests information from the employer about the whistleblower, the question arises whether the employer can refuse the information categorically due to ongoing internal investigations against the affected person. One could draw a parallel conclusion with regard to the criminal procedural legal situation. There, one would have to ask the question whether providing the identity of the whistleblower thwarts the protection of the ongoing investigations and additionally the protection of the (possibly) to be protected whistleblower. In this specific scenario, however, the access to information cannot depend on whether the affected person might excessively proceed against the whistleblower, attack him personally or put him at a disadvantage due to existing power structures. If it were solely about the risk of impairing internal investigations, this would not do justice to the protection of the whistleblower. A disclosure at such an early stage would likely run counter to the protection of the whistleblower if it later turns out that the whistleblower has reported accurate information in a sincere manner.[37]

The argument that the employer may refuse to provide information to the affected person because he has special duties of care towards the whistleblower as his employee is to be neglected. Because on the one hand, the employment law

---

[32] Under German law this is enshrined in Sec. 169a German Criminal Procedural Code (StPO).

[33] Under German law this is enshrined in Sec. 147 para. 2 sentence 1 German Criminal Procedural Code (StPO).

[34] Schmitt (2024), Sec. 147, para. 25.

[35] Cf. also European Data Protection Supervisor, Guidelines on processing personal information within a whistleblowing procedure (2016), para. 20.

[36] Regional Court (LG) Bochum, Dec. of 16.3.2016 – II-6 Qs 1/16.

[37] Quaas (2023), Art. 12, para. 35; Franck (2022) Art. 12, para. 28; Paal (2021) Art. 12, para. 52.

duties of care apply both to the whistleblower as an employee and to the affected person as an employee, so that the duty of care argues for both sides. On the other hand, the relationship between the employer and the whistleblower is not of special privilege, hence not comparable to the relationship between a lawyer and a client.[38]

Even during the internal investigations, a balancing of interests from Art. 6 para. 1 subpara. 1. f) GDPR is necessary. If there are no serious arguments against the whistleblower at this point, the balance should be in favour of the whistleblower. Even if one were to allow a summary examination of the substantive information on the hint in addition to the risk of thwarting, this would probably not adequately protect the whistleblower. At the same time, it should regularly be reasonable for the affected person to wait until the internal investigations are completed.

In order for the requirements of the case-related balancing to be actually complied with and also easier to review in court later, the employer should have a duty to provide reasons if he refuses to disclose the identity of the whistleblower. In addition, Art. 12 para. 4 GDPR stipulates the duty of the controller to justify the refusal of information. Also with regard to the denial of file inspection,[39] the public prosecutor's office has a duty to provide reasons.[40]

However, this obligation to provide reasons may not always be easy to fulfil in practice, unless simply referring to the ongoing investigations in a blanket manner. On the one hand, the affected person has a right to know why his right to information is restricted. On the other hand, the explanations of the employer, which are supposed to protect the whistleblower, should not trigger the opposite. Therefore, the employer must always consider that the identity of the whistleblower is not indirectly revealed by the justification.

4.4.2 Dilatory Right to Refuse Information in the Context of Data Protection Deadlines

If there is a time-limited right to refuse information until the conclusion of the investigations, this probably regularly collides with the data protection information deadlines. According to Art. 12 para. 3 sentence 1 GDPR, the desired information must be provided within one month. This one-month period may be extended by a further two months according to Art. 12 para. 3 sentence 2 GDPR if this is necessary considering the complexity of the case. Considering the above-mentioned balancing criteria, complexity can regularly be assumed in such cases. But even if one assumes that the employer may make use of the three-month

[38] Higher Regional Labour Court (LAG) Baden-Württemberg Judg. of 20.12.2018–17 Sa 11/18, para. 229.

[39] Under German law this is enshrined in Sec. 147 para. 2 sentence 1 German Criminal Procedural Code (StPO).

[40] Under German law this is enshrined in Sec. 34 German Criminal Procedural Code (StPO).

period, the internal investigations are unlikely to be fully completed within this time. At the same time, the three-month period is the absolute maximum, which the employer cannot extend further. A suspension of deadlines is not provided for in the GDPR.

However, the deadlines from Art. 12 para. 3 sentence 1 GDPR, according to an agreeable opinion, do not represent processing deadlines, but only refer to a reaction to the status of the application.[41] Furthermore, in the case of the dilatory right to refuse information, the substantive answer should not refer to the result of the internal investigations, which is not yet available, but rather to the examination of the possibility of waiting. In this respect, the monthly deadlines should be adhered to.

4.4.3 Right to Refuse Access Due to a Confidentiality Agreement

Basically, even in the case of a confidentiality agreement with the whistleblower, the basic weighting of interests remains, namely, that information can only be refused in exceptional cases, not due to general confidentiality agreements. The employer cannot simply refuse a right to information by invoking a confidentiality agreement with the whistleblower. The LAG Baden-Württemberg has already recognised that it can basically be a legitimate interest to keep the identity of a whistleblower confidential if the employer promises special confidentiality to the whistleblower for the purpose of clarifying internal misconduct.[42]

When assessing confidentiality interests, the underlying accusation plays a particularly important role. Especially in the area of corruption, a confidentiality agreement may actually be necessary. Yet, there are situations where, even with an existing confidentiality agreement, the interest in confidentiality must take a back seat to the interest in information. According to the Regional Labout Court (LAG) Baden-Württemberg, this can be the case if the whistleblower has given incorrect information knowingly or negligently. With regard to the obligation to provide reasons, the court therefore demands a detailed justification with reference to the facts in the specific individual case. A blanket justification is out of the question. In case of a refusal to disclose the identity of the whistleblower, the employer is to disclose, to explain and to prove.

In conclusion, the court is to be agreed with. However, practical questions remain open. The court's view is convincing in terms of content because the conflict of interest, according to the legislative intention, is regularly to be resolved in favour of the person seeking information, while the protection of the whistleblower rarely prevails. However, effective whistleblower protection, according to

---

[41] Dix (2019) Art. 15, para. 35.

[42] Higher Regional Labour Court (LAG) Baden-Württemberg Judg. of 20.12.2018–17 Sa 11/18, para. 229.

the court's statements, is likely to be realised only after the investigations have been completed. Because even if the accuracy of the information is important, it will hardly be possible, in practice, to evaluate this before the investigations are completed and thus to allow the whistleblower to be protected.

The employer must also justify the rejection of access at this point. But here too, there may be difficulties, in practice, in not making such statements in the justification that indirectly reveal the identity of the whistleblower.

4.5 Overall Tendency Towards Whistleblower Protection

The previous analysis has shown that the denial of the right of access must be well founded and even the temporary denial of the right of access must be explained to the data subject. This seems to carve out the tendency towards the right of access rather than the whistleblower protection, when balancing the interests. However, this is not that simple. In fact, a whistleblower is generally protected, unless he or she acts illegally namely to make willingly or knowingly false statements and slandering another person. In the other cases, the whistleblower may trust in his right to have his or her identity protected. Even so, one may hope for a further and nuanced guidance by courts especially the ECJ in that regard.[43]

References

Academic Articles and Contributions

Dendorfer-Ditges, R (2021) Munich lawyer's manual employment law. In: Moll, Wilhelm (ed) 5th edn

Dix A (2019) GDPR. In: Spiecker Gn, Döhmann, Indra, Papakonstantinou, Vagelis, Hornung, Gerrit, De Hert, Paul 1st edn

Franck L (2022) General data protection regulation – Federal data protection Act. In: Gola, Peter, Heckmann, Dirk 3rd edn

Gerdemann S, Colneric N (2021) The EU whistleblower directive and its transposition: Part I. Eur Lab Law J 2(12):193

Krieger H (2022) ECHR/German constitution. In: Dörr, Oliver, Grote, Rainer, Marauhn, Thilo, 3rd edn

Lühning T (2023) Auskunftsersuchen des Beschuldigten bei internen Ermittlungen Kriterien zur Interessenabwägung zwischen Daten- und Hinweisgeberschutz. Zd 136

Martinico G (2012) Is the European convention going to be 'Supreme'? A comparative-constitutional overview of ECHR and EU law before national courts. EJIL 2(23):401

Meyer F (2023) LuxLeaks, Cum-Ex & Co – neue Leitlinien des EGMR für Whistleblowing in transnationalen Kontexten und gesetzgeberischer Handlungsbedarf. 7JZ 78:26

[43] See a similar call for more internationally unified guidance for example: Yurttagül (2021), p. 293 et seq.

Mohn M (2022) Das Recht auf Auskunft nach Art. 15 DS-GVO und der Schutz des Hinweisgebers. Nza 17:1165

Nettesheim M (2023) ECHR European convention on human rights. In: Meyer-Ladewig J, Nettesheim Martin, von R Stefan, 5th edn

Paal B (2021) General data protection regulation federal data protection Act. In: Paal, Boris, Pauly, Daniel, 3rd edn

Petri D (2023) IT employment law. In: Kramer, Stefan, 3rd edn

Quaas S (2023) Beck's online commentary data protection law. In: Wolff, Heinrich A Brinck, Stefan, Beck's 45th edn

Schmitt B (2024) Code of German criminal procedure (StPO). In: Meyer-Goßner Lutz Schmitt Bertram 67th edn

Schubert C (2024) Commentary on European labour law. In: Franzen M Gallner I Oetker H 5th edn

Trojsi A (2024) The confirmed, indeed reinforced, centrality of the GDPR for the protection of workers' Personal rights in the light of subsequent EU Legislative Acts, 2 Italian Labour Law e-Journal 17, p. 355

Wessing J (2023) Beck's online commentary on the German criminal procedural code (StPO). In: Graf J (ed) 48th edn

Yurttagül H (2021) Whistleblower protection by the council of Europe, the European court of human rights and the European union

Court Decisions

ECtHR Judg. of 12.2.2008 – 14,277/04, Guja against Moldova

ECtHR Judg. of 16.02.2021 – 23,922/19, Gawlik against Liechtenstein

ECtHR Judg. of 5.9.2017 – 61,496/08, Barbulescu against Romania

German Constitutional Court (BVerfG) Dec. of 2.7.2001 – 1 BvR 2049/00

Higher Regional Labour Court (LAG) Baden-Württemberg Judg. of 20.12.2018 – 17 Sa 11/18

Regional Court (LG) Bochum, Dec. of 16.3.2016 – II-6 Qs 1/16, also in: NStZ 2016, p. 500

Official Documents

Article 29 Working Party, Opinion 1/2006 on the application of EU data protection rules to internal whistleblowing schemes in the fields of accounting, internal accounting controls, auditing matters, fight against bribery, banking and financial crime, 00195/06/EN

Committee of Ministers of the Council of Europe, Recommendation CM/Rec(2014)7 on the protection of whistleblowers of 30.4.2014

European Data Protection Supervisor (2016) Guidelines on processing personal information within a whistleblowing procedure. Available at https://edps.europa.eu/sites/edp/files/publication/16-07-18_whistleblowing_guidelines_en.pdf. Accessed on 14 Sept 2025

Chapter 5
Conclusion and Outlook

Overall, it is easy to conclude that the data protection right of access is generally designed as a strong claim that lies at the heart of the data subjects' rights under the General Data Protection Regulation (GDPR). On various occasions, the European Court of Justice (ECJ) confirmed that only a stark and robust right of access enables the data subject to control his or her data and make use of the other rights under the GDPR such as the right to correction, erasure, or to data portability.

Nevertheless, at least equally strong is the right to whistleblower protection. In many cases, the interest in preserving the confidentiality of the whistleblower's identity is likely to prevail when balancing it with the right of access. The whistleblower protection and the interest in confidentiality is likely to be strong enough as long as the whistleblower provides correct information and acts in good faith with regard to the reported information, the information relates to violations of the law, and the whistleblower is pursuing pure interests by his or her report.

Since the legal deadline for implementing the Whistleblower Protection Directive expired on 17 December 2021, the EU Member States by now have enacted whistleblower legislation in their national laws. As the Whistleblower Protection Directive leaves the member states some room for specifications, these aspects have the potential to be further regulated by national laws. The debates now mostly centre on the quality of the transpositions of the directive into the respective national laws. In March 2025, the European Court of Justice (ECJ) imposed multimillion-euro lump-sum fines on five member states (Germany, Luxembourg, Czech Republic, Estonia, and Hungary), for having transposed the directive either too late or not at all.[1] NGOs such as Transparency International argue that several Member States still fall short of at least one minimum whistle-blower protection standard, particularly on anonymity, and a failure of adopting the

[1] ECJ, Press Release (2025).

S. Koloßa, *Whistleblower Protection and the Right of Access*, SpringerBriefs in Law,
https://doi.org/10.1007/978-3-032-04817-2_5

directive's optional higher safeguards.[2] As the example of Germany and the German Whistleblower Protection Law[3] shows, the aspect of balancing the right to whistleblower protection with the right of access has been entirely left untouched by the legislator. Other states such as France do not specifically regulate this aspect in their laws.[4]

In the area of data protection law, the right of access is currently re-examined. The European Data Protection Board (EDPB) has found in its report on the implementation of the right of access adopted in 2025 that organisations still limit internal searches to a few databases, neglect internal guidelines, and respond with generic templates.[5] The report urges controllers to handle each request case-by-case and to document their search logic. In parallel, the European Data Protection Supervisor (EDPS) highlighted similar weaknesses inside EU institutions—fragmented record-keeping and difficulties categorising requests—and promised closer audits.[6]

Across all these strands, a common theme dominates current discussion: Europe recognises whistleblowing and the right of access as essential (democratic) tools, yet their promise will depend on better enforcement mechanisms, clearer procedural guarantees and cultures of openness inside both public bodies and private organisations. Ultimately, it remains to be seen whether the legislators, the data protection authorities, or the courts will give more detailed guidelines leading to a more legally coherent environment.

Meanwhile, businesses face their own compliance race: Germany's whistleblower protection law and similar national acts oblige firms with more than 50 employees to run confidential internal channels, with fines of up to €50,000 for non-compliance after December 2023, prompting a market in digital speak-up tools and fresh guidance from advisory firms on harmonising cross-border procedures. As the member states host legal frameworks, current discussion has shifted from formal transposition to practical effectiveness, most crucially how to foster trust so that insiders use internal systems before turning to regulators or the press, and how to give investigators the resources to follow up on the rising number of external reports. Finally, another aim for corporations is to automize standard procedure for further reliance and raising efficiencies of internal procedures. However, this is only possible with more reliable legal standards that may be technically executed.

[2] Transparency International (2024).

[3] Hinweisgeberschutzgesetz (HinSchG).

[4] Cf. e.g. French Law No. 2022–401.

[5] EDPB Report (2025).

[6] EDPS Statement (2025).

References

European Court of Justice Press, Release No. 29/25 6 Mar 2025
European Data Protection Board (2024) Coordinated Enforcement Action, Implementation of the right of access by controllers. 16 Jan 2025
European Data Protection Supervisor Coordinated Enforcement Action: EDPS findings highlight challenges on right of access to personal data. 20 Jan 2025
Transparency International Report EU whistleblower protection: Falling short when it matters most. 16 Dec 2024

Made in the USA
Monee, IL
13 September 2026

62975226R00057